An Introduction to Fixed Income Securities

An Introduction to Fixed Income Securities

Anuk Teasdale
Moorad Choudhry

YieldCurve.publishing

SURREY, ENGLAND

YieldCurve.publishing
PO Box 101, East Horsley, Surrey KT24 5EU England
A division of YieldCurve.com

Published by YieldCurve.publishing, Surrey, England

A member of the YieldCurve.com Associates

First published 2003

British Library Cataloguing in Publication Data
A catalogue record for this book is available from the British Library

ISBN 0 9545447 06

Typeset by Tradespools, Somerset, England
Printed and bound by the Antony Rowe Group, Wiltshire, England

TABLE OF CONTENTS

PREFACE

This book is aimed specifically at beginners, or newcomers to the bond markets who require a succinct but comprehensive grounding in fixed income securities and some of their derivatives. We present the key principles in accessible style.

The bond markets are an important part of the global financial markets, and a vital conduit through which capital is raised and invested. One characteristic of the markets is the introduction of ever more sophisticated financial engineering techniques, such that the bond markets today comprise trading in a large variety of structures. Investment banks can tailor packages to suit the most esoteric of requirements for their customers, so that bond cash flows and the hedging instruments available for holders of bonds can be far removed from the conventional fixed interest instruments that originally made up the market. Instruments are now available that will suit the needs of virtually all users of the financial markets, whether they are investors or borrowers.

The purpose of this book is to provide an introductory description and analysis of bond instruments. We consider basic "plain vanilla" bonds and elementary bond mathematics. We also look at two very commonly-encountered derivatives of bonds, interest-rate swaps and bond futures, and their uses. Readers who wish to investigate the markets beyond the depth afforded here may wish to consult Moorad Choudhry's book *The Bond and Money Markets: Strategy, Trading, Analysis*, published by Butterworth Heinemann.

This book is aimed at those with little or no previous understanding of or exposure to the bond markets. This includes beginners in front office, middle office and back office banking and fund management departments. Others including corporate treasurers, risk management and legal department staff may also find the contents useful.

Further information is available at the fixed income research website

www.YieldCurve.com

ABOUT THE AUTHORS

Anuk Teasdale is a research associate and senior partner at YieldCurve.com.

Moorad Choudhry has over 15 years experience in investment banking in the City of London and was a bond trader at ABN Amro Hoare Govett and Hambros Bank Limited. He is a Visiting Professor at the Department of Economics, Finance and International Business, London Metropolitan University and a Fellow of the Securities Institute.

1 Introduction

Those who watch television news bulletins in the UK, both terrestrial and some satellite programmes, will be familiar with the cursory bit, delivered either at the end or during the "business" slot, when the newscaster informs viewers where the main stock market index closed that day and where key foreign exchange rates closed at. There is no mention of bond yields. This is a pity, because government bond yields give a much better and more reliable indication of the economy than stock indices. In the United States, some television news bulletins do inform the viewer at what yield the Treasury long bond closed at. This recognises that bond prices are affected directly by economic and political events, and yield levels on certain government bonds are fundamental indicators of the economy. The yield level on the US Treasury long bond reflects the market's view on US interest rates, inflation, public sector debt and economic growth. Reporting the bond yield level reflects the importance of the bond market to a country's economy, as important as the level of the equity stock market. Under the same logic, it would make sense if news programmes in the UK started to inform us at what yield the 10-year benchmark gilt yield closed at, and what this represented as a change on say, last week's closing yield.

Bonds and shares form part of the *capital markets*. Shares are *equity capital* while bonds are *debt capital*. So bonds are a form of debt, much like how a bank loan is a form of debt. Unlike bank loans, however, bonds can be *traded* in a market. A bond is a debt capital market instrument issued by a borrower, who is then required to repay to the lender/investor the amount borrowed plus interest, over a specified period of time. Bonds are also known as *fixed income* instruments, or *fixed interest* instruments in the sterling markets. Usually bonds are considered to be those debt securities with terms to maturity of over one year. Debt issued with a maturity of less than one year is considered to be *money market* debt. There are many different types of bonds that can be issued. The most common bond is the *conventional* (or *plain vanilla* or *bullet*) bond. This is a bond paying regular (annual or semi-annual) interest at a fixed rate over a fixed period to maturity or redemption, with the return of *principal* (the par or nominal value of the bond) on the maturity date. All other bonds will be variations on this.

A bond is therefore a financial contract, in effect an IOU, from the person or body that has issued the bond. Unlike shares or equity capital, bonds carry no ownership privileges. An investor who has purchased a bond and thereby lent money to an institution will have no voice in the affairs of that institution and no vote at the annual general meeting. The bond remains an interest-bearing obligation of the issuer until it is repaid, which is usually the maturity date of the bond. The issuer can be anyone from a private individual to a sovereign government.

There is a wide range of participants involved in the bond markets. We can group them broadly into borrowers and investors, plus the institutions and individuals who are part of the business of bond trading. Borrowers access the bond markets as part of their financing requirements; hence borrowers can include sovereign governments, local authorities, public sector organisations and corporates. Virtually all businesses operate with a financing structure that is a mixture of debt and equity finance. The debt finance may well contain a form of bond finance, so it is easy to see what an important part of the global economy the bond markets are.

The different types of bonds in the market reflect the different types of issuers and their respective requirements. Some bonds are safer investments than others. The advantage of bonds to an investor is that they represent a fixed source of current income, with an assurance of repayment of the loan on maturity. Bonds issued by developed country governments are deemed to be guaranteed investments in that the final repayment is virtually certain. In the event of default of the issuing entity, bondholders rank above shareholders for compensation payments. There is lower risk associated with bonds compared to shares as an investment, and therefore almost invariably a lower return in the long term.

We can look up detail on bonds in our daily paper.

Figure 1.1 is an extract from the *Financial Times* for 16 August 2002, showing prices and yields for United Kingdom government bonds or *gilts*. Each bond is

UK GILTS - cash market

Aug 15	Notes	... Yield ... Int	Red	Price £	+ or −	... 52 week ... High	Low
Shorts" (Lives up to Five Years)							
Tr 9¾pc '02		9.73	4.20	100.17	−.02	104.98	100.17
Tr 8pc '02–6		7.96	3.87	100.55	−.03	120.76	100.55
Ex 9pc '02	✣	8.88	3.85	101.30	−.04	105.38	101.30
Tr 11¾pc '03–7	✣	11.38	3.98	103.29	−.08	109.62	103.29
Cn 9¾pc '03	✣	9.38	4.10	103.99	−.11	108.86	103.99
Tr 8pc '03		7.74	3.77	103.36	−.12	106.39	103.29
Tr 10pc '03		9.40	3.86	106.33	−.17	110.70	106.21
Tr 12½pc '03–5	✣	11.32	3.94	110.44	−.21	116.69	110.42
Tr 6½pc '03		6.30	3.95	103.22	−.21	105.24	102.41
Tr 13½pc '04–8	✣	11.78	4.03	114.63	−.31	121.09	114.39
Tr 10pc '04	✣	9.10	4.09	109.90xd	−.28	114.62	109.35
Tr 5pc '04		4.92	4.02	101.69	−.29	102.52	99.74
Fnd 3½pc '99–4		3.53	3.98	99.13	−.24	99.47	95.80
Cn 9½pc '04	✣	8.56	4.20	110.97	−.39	114.79	109.95
Tr 6¾pc '04		6.40	4.20	105.47	−.38	107.61	103.79
Cn 9½pc '05		8.42	4.37	112.80	−.46	116.62	111.37
Ex 10½pc '05	✣	8.95	4.44	117.35	−.53	122.02	115.73
Tr 8½pc '05		7.57	4.45	112.33	−.54	115.68	110.29
Tr 7¾pc '06		6.93	4.53	111.84	−.63	114.60	109.11
Cn 9¾pc '06	✣	8.14	4.55	119.85	−.67	123.81	117.24
Tr 7½pc '06		6.73	4.53	111.51	−.67	114.24	108.68
Five to Ten Years							
Tr 8½pc '07		7.26	4.59	117.01	−.75	120.39	113.96
Tr 7¼pc '07		6.45	4.60	112.37	−.78	115.11	108.88
Tr 5pc '08		4.90	4.60	101.97	−.75	102.72	99.48
Tr 5½pc '08–12		5.24	4.56	104.96	−.67	107.03	100.96
Tr 9pc '08	✣	7.32	4.66	122.97	−.92	127.06	119.44
Tr 8pc '09	✣	6.66	4.66	120.04	−.97	123.89	115.71
Tr 5¾pc '09		5.39	4.65	106.77	−.92	109.01	102.25
Tr 6¼pc '10		5.64	4.66	110.78	−1.00	113.58	105.88
Cn 9pc Ln '11		6.86	4.69	131.11	−1.15	136.49	126.13
Ten to Fifteen Years							
Tr 7¾pc '12–15		6.37	4.86	121.64xd	−1.09	125.65	116.44
Tr 5pc '12		4.87	4.66	102.62	−1.01	105.10	97.47
Tr 9pc '12	✣	6.71	4.69	134.03	−1.20	138.79	128.43
Tr 8pc '13		6.22	4.67	128.62	−1.28	132.78	122.42
Tr 5pc '14		4.85	4.67	103.01	−1.16	104.17	100.76
Tr 8pc '15		6.04	4.69	132.54	−1.42	137.03	125.28
Over Fifteen Years							
Ex 12pc '13–17	✣	7.33	4.69	163.64	−1.55	170.34	156.67
Tr 8¾pc '17		6.11	4.71	143.19xd	−1.60	148.65	134.98
Tr 8pc '21		5.64	4.64	141.86	−1.82	147.48	132.30
Tr 5pc '25		4.72	4.58	105.87	−1.65	110.38	97.11
Tr 6pc '28		4.91	4.54	122.24	−1.91	127.99	111.75
Tr 4¼pc '32		4.42	4.49	96.06	−1.70	101.44	86.77
Undated							
Cons 4pc	✣	4.94	–	80.99	−1.90	85.72	71.57
War Ln 3½pc		4.71	–	74.31	−1.61	78.34	65.09
Cn 3½pc '61 Aft	✣	4.41	–	79.31	−1.90	83.95	68.93
Tr 3pc '66 Aft	✣	5.29	–	56.71	−1.26	59.81	50.52
Cons 2½pc	✣	4.84	–	51.66	−1.25	54.76	45.55
Tr 2½pc		4.86	–	51.49	−1.02	54.36	45.61

	Notes	... Yield ... (1)	(2)	Price £	+ or −	... 52 week ... High	Low
Index-Linked	(b)						
2½pc '03	(78.8)	–	0.83	222.23	−.04	222.27	216.46
4⅜pc '04	(135.6)	1.12	1.67	134.76	−.04	135.77	132.09
2pc '06	(69.5)	1.75	2.05	248.28	−.13	248.41	238.71
2½pc '09	(78.8)	2.04	2.22	223.20	−.18	223.38	214.88
2½pc '11	(74.6)	2.11	2.25	236.41	−.17	236.74	226.77
2½pc '13	(89.2)	2.11	2.22	198.95xd	−.20	199.86	189.85
2½pc '16	(81.6)	2.07	2.18	219.84	−.11	221.45	207.99
2½pc '20	(83.0)	2.04	2.12	220.01	−.10	222.24	205.93
2½pc '24	(97.7)	1.99	2.06	190.73	−.06	193.89	176.91
4⅛pc '30	(135.1)	1.96	2.02	184.92	−.38	190.18	171.84
2pc '35	(173.6)	1.91	1.96	100.32	−.31	100.63	94.06

Prospective real redemption rate on projected inflation of (1) 5% and (2) 3%. (b) Figures in parentheses show RPI base for indexing (ie 8 months prior to issue) and have been adjusted to reflect rebasing of RPI to 100 in January 1987. Conversion factor 3.945. RPI for Dec 2001: 173.4 and for July 2002: 175.9.

● Source: Debt Management Office (DMO). All UK Gilts are tax-free to non-residents on application. xd Ex dividend. Closing mid-prices are shown in pounds per £100 nominal of stock. Int yield: Interest yield. Red yield: Gross redemption yield.
Prospective real Index-Linked redemption yields are calculated by HSBC Bank plc from GEMMA closing prices. ✣ Indicative price. Gilts "runners", the benchmarks and most liquid stocks, are shown in bold type.

Gilt strips

	Price	Aug 15 Yield	Wk ago yield	Mth ago yield
7.25% '07	78.39	4.60	4.54	4.92
8% '15	53.78	4.72	4.76	4.99
8% '21	42.30	4.63	4.70	4.90

Source: DMO. See www.dmo.gov.uk

Gilt spreads - zero-coupon yield curve

	15-Aug	14-Aug	Wk Ago	Mth Ago
5 yrs v 2 yrs	46	45	51	36
10 yrs v 5 yrs	12	15	21	4
20 yrs v 10 yrs	-12	-11	-8	-13

Source: UBS Warburg, Gilt Strategy Perspectives.

Figure 1.1: UK gilts prices, 16 August 2002. © *Financial Times.* Reproduced with permission.

```
16:53 KING & SHAXSON BOND BROKERS          PAGE 1 / 3
      UK Gilt Prices
      Full List          Close    Current   Change    Gry     Time
  1) UKT  9³₄  02        100.120   100.120            3.61    8:00
  2) UKT  8    03        103.290   103.290            3.81    16:40
  3) UKT  10   03        106.230   106.230            3.90    16:40
  4) UKT  6¹₂  03        103.150   103.150            3.98    16:40
  5) UKT  5    04        101.610   101.610            4.06    16:40
  6) UKT  6³₄  04        105.350   105.350            4.24    16:24
  7) UKT  9¹₂  05        112.630   112.630            4.42    16:24
  8) UKT  8¹₂  05        112.150   112.150            4.49    16:24
  9) UKT  7³₄  06        111.640   111.640            4.57    16:24
 10) UKT  8    02/06     100.490   100.490            3.82    16:40
 11) UKT  7¹₂  06        111.320   111.320            4.57    16:24
 12) UKT  6¹₂  07        116.780   116.780            4.64    16:30
 13) UKT  7¹₄  07        112.150   112.150            4.64    16:24
 14) UKT  5    08        101.790   101.790            4.63    16:40
 15) UKT  5 ³₄ 09        106.590   106.590            4.67    16:24


            Prices shown are indication only.
*Important*
            Prices will soon only be available to registered users.
            Contact KSBB on 020 7776 2630
Australia 61 2 9777 8600      Brazil 5511 3048 4500      Europe 44 20 7330 7500      Germany 49 69 920410
Hong Kong 852 2977 6000 Japan 81 3 3201 8900 Singapore 65 212 1000 U.S. 1 212 318 2000  Copyright 2002 Bloomberg L.P.
                                                                      G797-57-0 19-Aug-02 16:53:38
Bloomberg
PROFESSIONAL
```

Figure 1.2: King & Shaxson Bond Brokers Ltd, gilts page, 19 August 2002.
© Bloomberg L.P. © Old Mutual plc. Used with permission.

shown with its price from the day before, as well as two yield measure, the "Int" yield and the "Red" yield. These stand for "interest" and "redemption" respectively and we will show what these mean a little later. There are also separate tables for different types of gilts, *Undated*, *Index-linked* and *Strips*. These are gilts that have special features associated with their coupon and return.

Market professionals obtain their bond data from electronic news media. Figure 1.2 shows the King & Shaxson Bond Brokers Limited page "KSBB" as it appears on the Bloomberg news system; this was the page for 19 August 2002. King & Shaxson is a leading broker in the gilts market. The page shows closing prices for the leading stocks. It also shows the gross redemption yield at the indicated price and the change on the previous day's closing price.

In chapter 2 we look at some important features of bonds.[1] This is followed by an introduction to bond futures and interest-rate swaps, two derivative instruments that are commonly encountered in the bond markets.

---

[1] Bonds are also known as *fixed income* instruments or, in the sterling markets, as *fixed interest* instruments. This refers to the rate of interest payable on the loan represented by the bond, despite that for a great many bonds the rate of interest is not *fixed* at all. . . .

2 A Primer on Bond Basics

In this chapter we review the key features of bond instruments.

2.1 Description

We have said that a bond is a debt instrument, usually paying a fixed rate of interest over a fixed period of time. Therefore a bond is a collection of cash flows and this is illustrated at Figure 2.1. In our hypothetical example the bond is a six-year issue that pays fixed interest payments of C% of the *nominal* value on an annual basis. In the sixth year there is a final interest payment and the loan proceeds represented by the bond are also paid back, known as the maturity proceeds. The amount raised by the bond issuer is a function of the price of the bond at issue, which we have labelled here as the issue proceeds.

The upward facing arrow represents the cash flow paid and the downward facing arrows are the cash flows received by the bond investor. The cash flow diagram for a six-year bond that had a 5% fixed interest rate, known as a 5% *coupon*, would show interest payments of £5 per every £100 of bonds, with a final payment of £105 in the sixth year, representing the last coupon payment and the redemption payment. Again, the amount of funds raised per £100 of bonds depends on the price of the bond on the day it is first issued, and we will look further into this later. If our example bond paid its coupon on a semi-annual basis, the cash flows would be £2.50 every six months until the final redemption payment of £102.50.

Let us examine some of the key features of bonds.

2.1.1 Type of issuer

A primary distinguishing feature of a bond is its issuer. The nature of the issuer will affect the way the bond is viewed in the market. There are four issuers of bonds: sovereign governments and their agencies, local government authorities, supranational bodies such as the World Bank, and corporations. Within the corporate bond market there is a wide range of issuers, each with differing abilities to satisfy their contractual obligations to investors. The largest bond markets are those of sovereign borrowers, the government bond markets. The United Kingdom government issues *gilts*. In the United States government bonds are known as *Treasury Notes* and *Treasury Bonds*, or simply *Treasuries*.

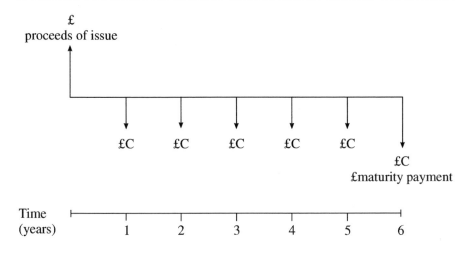

Figure 2.1: Cash flows associated with a six-year annual coupon bond.

2.1.2 Term to maturity

The *term to maturity* of a bond is the number of years after which the issuer will repay the obligation. During the term the issuer will also make periodic interest payments on the debt. The *maturity* of a bond refers to the date that the debt will cease to exist, at which time the issuer will redeem the bond by paying the principal. The practice in the market is often to refer simply to a bond's "term" or "maturity". The provisions under which a bond is issued may allow either the issuer or investor to alter a bond's term to maturity after a set notice period, and such bonds need to be analysed in a different way. The term to maturity is an important consideration in the make-up of a bond. It indicates the time period over which the bondholder can expect to receive the coupon payments and the number of years before the principal will be paid in full. The bond's *yield* also depends on the term to maturity. Finally, the price of a bond will fluctuate over its life as yields in the market change and as it approaches maturity. As we will discover later, the *volatility* of a bond's price is dependent on its maturity; assuming other factors constant, the longer a bond's maturity the greater the price volatility resulting from a change in market yields.

2.1.3 Principal and coupon rate

The *principal* of a bond is the amount that the issuer agrees to repay the bondholder on the maturity date. This amount is also referred to as the *redemption value, maturity value, par value* or *face amount*, or simply *par*. The *coupon rate* or *nominal rate* is the interest rate that the issuer agrees to pay each year. The annual amount of the interest payment made is called the *coupon*. The coupon rate multiplied by the principal of the bond provides the cash amount of the coupon. For example a bond with a 7% coupon rate and a principal of £1,000,000 will pay annual interest of £70,000. In the United Kingdom, United States and Japan the usual practice is for the issuer to pay the coupon in two semi-annual instalments. For bonds issued in European markets and the Eurobond market coupon payments are made annually. On rare occasions one will encounter bonds that pay interest on a quarterly basis. All bonds make periodic interest payments except for *zero-coupon bonds*. These bonds allow a holder to realise interest by being sold substantially below their principal value. The bonds are redeemed at par, with the interest amount then being the difference between the principal value and the price at which the bond was sold. We will explore zero-coupon bonds in greater detail later.

2.1.4 Currency

Bonds can be issued in virtually any currency. The largest volume of bonds in the global markets is denominated in US dollars; other major bond markets are denominated in euros, Japanese yen and sterling, and liquid markets also exist in Australian, New Zealand and Canadian dollars, Swiss francs and other major currencies. The currency of issue may impact on a bond's attractiveness and liquidity which is why borrowers in developing countries often elect to issue in a currency other than their home currency, for example dollars, as this will make it easier to place the bond with investors. If a bond is aimed solely at a country's domestic investors it is more likely that the borrower will issue in the home currency.

2.2   Bond issuers

2.2.1 Issuers and participants

In most countries government expenditure exceeds the level of government income received through taxation. This shortfall is made up by government borrowing and bonds are issued to finance the government's debt. The core of any domestic capital market is usually the government bond market, which also forms the benchmark for all other borrowing.

Gilts are identified by their coupon rate and year of maturity; they are also given names such as *Treasury* or *Exchequer*. There is no significance attached to any particular name – all gilts are equivalent irrespective of their name. From Figure 1.1 in Chapter 1 we see that the $5\frac{3}{4}\%$ 2009 stock closing price from the day before was 106.77, which means £106.77 of par value. (Remember that par is the lump sum paid at maturity.) This price represents a *gross redemption yield* of 4.65%. If we pay £106.77 per £100 of stock today, we will receive £100 per £100 of stock on maturity. At first sight this appears to imply we will lose money, however we also receive coupon payments every six months, which for this bond is £2.875 per £100 nominal of stock. Also from Figure 1.1 we see the change in price from the day before for each gilt; in the case of the $5\frac{3}{4}\%$ 2009 the price was down 0.92 from the previous day's closing price.

Government agencies also issue bonds. Such bonds are virtually as secure as government bonds. In the United States agencies include the Federal National Mortgage Association. Local authorities issue bonds as part of financing for roads, schools, hospitals and other capital projects.

Corporate borrowers issue bonds both to raise finance for major projects and also to cover ongoing and operational expenses. Corporate finance is a mixture of debt and equity and a specific capital project will often be financed as a mixture of both.

2.2.2 Capital market participants

The debt capital markets exist because of the financing requirements of governments and corporates. The source of capital is varied, but the total supply of funds in a market is made up of personal or household savings, business savings and increases in the overall money supply. Growth in the money supply is a function of the overall state of the economy, and interested readers may wish to consult the reference list at the end of this chapter which includes several standard economic texts. Individuals save out of their current income for future consumption, while business savings represent retained earnings. The entire savings stock represents the capital available in a market. As we saw in the preface, however, the requirements of savers and borrowers differ significantly, in that savers have a short-term investment horizon while borrowers prefer to take a longer-term view. The "constitutional weakness" of what would otherwise be unintermediated financial markets led, from an early stage, to the development of financial intermediaries.

Financial intermediaries

In its simplest form a financial intermediary is a *broker* or *agent*. Today we would classify the broker as someone who acts on behalf of the borrower or lender, buying or selling a bond as instructed. However intermediaries originally acted between borrowers and lenders in placing funds as required. A broker would not simply on-lend funds that have been placed with it, but would accept deposits and make loans as required by its customers. This resulted in the first banks.

A *retail bank* deals mainly with the personal financial sector and small businesses, and in addition to loans and deposits also provides cash transmission services. A retail bank is required to maintain a minimum cash reserve, to meet potential withdrawals, but the remainder of its deposit base can be used to make loans. This does not mean that the total size of its loan book is restricted to what it has taken in deposits: loans can also be funded in the wholesale market.

An *investment bank* will deal with governments, corporates and institutional investors. Investment banks perform an agency role for their customers and are the primary vehicle through which a corporate will borrow funds in the bond markets. This is part of the bank's corporate finance function. It will also act as wholesaler in the bond markets, a function known as *market making*. The bond issuing function of an investment bank, by which the bank will issue bonds on behalf of a customer and pass the funds raised to this customer, is known as *origination*. Investment banks will also carry out a range of other functions for institutional customers, including export finance, corporate advisory and fund management. Other financial intermediaries will trade not on behalf of clients but for their own *book*. These include *arbitrageurs* and speculators. Usually such market participants form part of investment banks.

Investors
There is a large variety of players in the bond markets, each trading some or all of the different instruments available to suit their own purposes. We can group the main types of investors according to the time horizon of their investment activity.

Short-term institutional investors
These include banks and building societies, money market fund managers, central banks and the treasury desks of some types of corporates. Such bodies are driven by short-term investment views, often subject to close guidelines, and will be driven by the total return available on their investments. Banks will have an additional requirement to maintain *liquidity*, often in fulfilment of regulatory authority rules, by holding a proportion of their assets in the form of easily-tradeable short-term instruments.

Long-term institutional investors
Typically these types of investors include pension funds and life assurance companies. Their investment horizon is long-term, reflecting the nature of their liabilities. Often they will seek to match these liabilities by holding long-dated bonds.

Mixed horizon institutional investors
This is possibly the largest category of investors and will include general insurance companies and most corporate bodies. Like banks and financial sector companies, they are also very active in the primary market, issuing bonds to finance their operations.

Market professionals

This category includes the banks and specialist financial intermediaries mentioned above, firms that one would not automatically classify as "investors" although they will also have an investment objective. Their time horizon will range from one day to the very long-term. They include the proprietary trading desks of investment banks, as well as bond market makers in securities houses and banks who are providing a service to their customers. Proprietary traders will actively position themselves in the market in order to gain trading profit, for example in response to their view on where they think interest rate levels are headed. These participants will trade direct with other market professionals and investors, or via brokers. Market makers or *traders* (also called *dealers* in the United States) are wholesalers in the bond markets; they make two-way prices in selected bonds. Firms will not necessarily be active market makers in all types of bonds; smaller firms often specialise in certain sectors. In a two-way quote the *bid price* is the price at which the market maker will buy stock, so it is the price the investor will receive when selling stock. The *offer price* or *ask price* is the price at which investors can buy stock from the market maker. As one might expect the bid price is always higher than the offer price, and it is this *spread* that represents the theoretical profit to the market maker. The bid-offer spread set by the market maker is determined by several factors, including supply and demand, and liquidity considerations for that particular stock, the trader's view on market direction and *volatility*, as well as that of the stock itself and the presence of any market intelligence. A large bid-offer spread reflects low liquidity in the stock, as well as low demand.

Markets

Markets are that part of the financial system where capital market transactions, including the buying and selling of securities, takes place. A market can describe a traditional stock exchange, a physical trading floor where securities trading occurs. Many financial instruments are traded over the telephone or electronically over computer links; these markets are known as *over-the-counter* (OTC) markets. A distinction is made between financial instruments of up to one year's maturity and instruments of over one year's maturity. Short-term instruments make up the *money market* while all other instruments are deemed to be part of the *capital market*. There is also a distinction made between the *primary market* and the *secondary market*. A new issue of bonds made by an investment bank on behalf of its client is made in the primary market. Such an issue can be a *public* offer, in which anyone can apply to buy the bonds, or a *private* offer where the customers of the investment bank are offered the stock. The secondary market is the market in which existing bonds and shares are subsequently traded.

2.3   World bond markets

The origin of the spectacular increase in the size of global financial markets was the rise in oil prices in the early 1970s. Higher oil prices stimulated the development of a sophisticated international banking system, as they resulted in large capital inflows to developed country banks from the oil-producing countries. A significant proportion of these capital flows were placed in *Eurodollar* deposits in major banks. The growing trade deficit and level of public borrowing in the United States also contributed. The last twenty years has seen tremendous growth in capital markets' volumes and trading. As capital controls were eased and exchange rates moved from fixed to floating, domestic capital markets became internationalised. Growth was assisted by the rapid advance in information technology and the widespread use of financial engineering techniques. Today we would think nothing of dealing in virtually any liquid currency bond in financial centres around the world, often at the touch of a button. Global bond issues, underwritten by the subsidiaries of the same banks, are commonplace. The ease with which transactions can be undertaken has also contributed to a very competitive market in liquid currency assets.

The world bond market has increased in size more than fifteen times in the last thirty years. As at the end of 2002 outstanding volume stood at over $21 trillion.

The market in US Treasury securities is the largest bond market in the world. Like the government bond markets in the UK, Germany, France and other developed economies, it is also very liquid and transparent. Table 2.1 lists the major government bond markets in the world; the US market makes up nearly half of the total. The Japanese market is second in size, followed by the German market. A large part of the government bond market is concentrated therefore in just a few countries. Government bonds are traded on major exchanges as well as

Country	Nominal value ($ billion)	Percentage (rounded)
United States	5,490	48.5
Japan	2,980	26.3
Germany	1,236	10.9
France	513	4.5
Canada	335	3.0
United Kingdom	331	2.9
Netherlands	253	2.2
Australia	82	0.7
Denmark	72	0.6
Switzerland	37	0.3
Total	11,329	100

Source: IFC 2003.

Table 2.1: Major government bond markets, December 2002.

over-the-counter. Generally OTC refers to trades that are not carried out on an exchange but directly between the counterparties. Bonds are also listed on exchanges, for example the NYSE had over 600 government issues listed on it at the end of 1998, with a total par value of $2.6 billion.

The corporate bond market varies in liquidity, depending on the currency and type of issuer of any particular bond. Outstanding volume as at the end of 2001 was over $7.5 trillion. Corporate bonds are also traded on exchanges and OTC. One of the most liquid corporate bond types is the *Eurobond*, which is an international bond issued and traded across national boundaries.

Companies finance their operations in a number of ways, from equity to short-term debt such as bank overdrafts. It is often advantageous for companies to fix longer-term finance, which is why bonds are so popular. Bonds are also attractive as a means of raising finance because the interest payable on them to investors is tax deductible for the company. Dividends on equity are not tax deductible. A corporate needs to get a reasonable mix of debt versus equity in its funding however, as a high level of interest payments will be difficult to service in times of recession or general market downturn. For this reason the market views unfavourably companies that have a high level of debt.

2.4   Non-conventional bonds

The definition of bonds given earlier in this chapter referred to conventional or *plain vanilla* bonds. There are many variations on vanilla bonds and we can introduce a few of them here.

Floating rate notes
The bond market is often referred to as the *fixed income* market, or the *fixed interest* market in the UK. Floating rate notes (FRNs) do not have a fixed coupon at all but instead link their interest payments to an external reference, such as the three-month bank lending rate. Bank interest rates will fluctuate constantly during the life of the bond and so an FRN's cash flows are not known with certainty. Usually FRNs pay a fixed margin or *spread* over the specified reference rate; occasionally the spread is not fixed and such a bond is known as a *variable rate note*. Because FRNs pay coupons based on the three-month or six-month bank rate they trade essentially as money market instruments.

Index-linked bonds
An index-linked bond has its coupon and redemption payment, or possibly just either one of these, linked to a specified index. When governments issue index-linked bonds the cash flows are linked to a price index such as consumer or commodity prices. Corporates have issued index-linked bonds that are connected to inflation or a stock market index.

Zero-coupon bonds

Certain bonds do not make any coupon payments at all and these are known as *zero-coupon bonds*. A zero-coupon bond or *strip* only has cash flow, the redemption payment, on maturity. If we assume that the maturity payment is say, £100 per cent or *par* the issue price will be at a discount to par. Such bonds are also known therefore as *discounted* bonds. The difference between the price paid on issue and the redemption payment is the interest realised by the bondholder. As we will discover when we look at strips this has certain advantages for investors, the main one being that there are no coupon payments to be invested during the bond's life. Both governments and corporates issue zero-coupon bonds. Conventional coupon-bearing bonds can be *stripped* into a series of individual cash flows, which would then trade as separate zero-coupon bonds. This is a common practice in government bond markets such as Treasuries or gilts where the borrowing authority does not actually issue strips, and they have to be created via the stripping process.

Securitised bonds

There is a large market in bonds whose interest and principal liability payments are backed by an underlying cash flow from another asset. By securitising the asset, a borrower can provide an element of cash flow backing to investors. For instance, a mortgage bank can use the cash inflows it receives on its mortgage book as asset backing for an issue of bonds. Such an issue would be known as a mortgage-backed security (MBS). Because residential mortgages rarely run to their full term, but are usually paid off earlier by homeowners, the notes that are backed by mortgages are also prepaid ahead of their legal final maturity. This feature means that MBS securities are not bullet bonds like vanilla securities, but are instead known as *amortising* bonds. Other asset classes that can be securitised include credit card balances, car loans, equipment lease receivables, nursing home receipts, museum or leisure park receipts, and so on.

Bonds with embedded options

Some bonds include a provision in their offer particulars that gives either the bondholder and/or the issuer an option to enforce early redemption of the bond. The most common type of option embedded in a bond is a *call feature*. A call provision grants the issuer the right to redeem all or part of the debt before the specified maturity date. An issuing company may wish to include such a feature as it allows it to replace an old bond issue with a lower coupon rate issue if interest rates in the market have declined. As a call feature allows the issuer to change the maturity date of a bond it is considered harmful to the bondholder's interests; therefore the market price of the bond at any time will reflect this. A call option is included in all asset-backed securities based on mortgages, for obvious reasons (asset-backed bonds are considered in a later chapter). A bond issue may also include a provision that allows the investor to change the maturity of the bond. This is known as a *put feature* and gives the bondholder the right to sell the bond back to the issuer at par on specified dates. The advantage to the bondholder is that if interest rates rise after the issue date, thus depressing the bond's value, the investor can realise par value by *putting* the bond back to the issuer. A *convertible* bond is an issue giving the bondholder the right to exchange the bond for a specified amount of shares (equity) in the issuing company. This feature allows the investor to take advantage of favourable movements in the price of the issuer's shares. The presence of embedded options in a bond makes valuation more complex compared to plain vanilla bonds.

2.5   Pricing a conventional bond

The principles of pricing in the bond market are exactly the same as those in other financial markets, which states that the price of any financial instrument is equal to the net present value today of all the future cash flows from the instrument. A bond price is expressed as per 100 nominal of the bond, or "per cent". So for example if the all-in price of a US dollar denominated bond is quoted as "98.00", this means that for every $100 nominal of the bond a buyer would pay $98. The interest rate or discount rate used as part of the present value (price) calculation is key to everything, as it reflects where the bond is trading in the market and how it is perceived by the market. All the determining factors that identify the bond – those discussed in this chapter and including the type of issuer, the maturity, the coupon and the currency – influence the interest rate at which a bond's cash flows are discounted, which will be roughly similar to the rate used for comparable bonds.

Since the price of a bond is equal to the present value of its cash flows, first we need to know the bond's cash flows before then determining the appropriate interest rate at which to discount the cash flows. We can then compute the price of the bond.

2.5.1 Bond cash flows

A vanilla bond's cash flows are the interest payments or coupons that are paid during the life of the bond, together with the final redemption payment. It is possible to determine the cash flows with certainty only for conventional bonds of a fixed maturity. So for example, we do not know with certainty what the cash flows are for bonds that have embedded options and can be redeemed early. The coupon payments for conventional bonds are made annually, semi-annually or quarterly. Some bonds pay monthly interest.

Therefore a conventional bond of fixed redemption date is made up of an annuity (its coupon payments) and the maturity payment. If the coupon is paid semi-annually, this means exactly half the coupon is paid as interest every six months. Both gilts and US Treasuries pay semi-annual coupons. For example, the 5% 2012 gilt has the following cash flows:

$$\text{Semi-annual coupon} = £100 \times 0.025$$
$$= £2.50$$
$$\text{Redemption payment} = £100$$

The bond was issued on 23 June 1999 and is redeemed on 7 March 2012, and pays coupon on 7 March and 7 September each year. So in 2002 the bond is made up of 20 cash flows of £2.50 and one of £100. The time between coupon payments for any bond is counted as 1 period, so there are 20 periods between the first and last cash flows for the gilt in our example. The maturity payment is received 20 periods from today.

2.5.2 The discount rate

The interest rate that is used to discount a bond's cash flows (therefore called the *discount* rate) is the rate required by the bondholder. It is therefore known as the bond's *yield*. The yield on the bond will be determined by the market and is the price demanded by investors for buying it, which is why it is sometimes called the bond's *return*. The required yield for any bond will depend on a number of political and economic factors, including what yield is being earned by other bonds of the same class. Yield is always quoted as an annualised interest rate, so that for a semi-annually paying bond exactly half of the annual rate is used to discount the cash flows.

2.5.3 Bond pricing

The *fair price* of a bond is the present value of all its cash flows. Therefore when pricing a bond we need to calculate the present value of all the coupon interest payments and the present value of the redemption payment, and sum these. The price of a conventional bond that pays annual coupons can therefore be given by (2.1).

$$\begin{aligned}
P &= \frac{C}{(1+r)} + \frac{C}{(1+r)^2} + \frac{C}{(1+r)^3} + \cdots\cdots + \frac{C}{(1+r)^N} + \frac{M}{(1+r)^N} \\
&= \sum_{n=1}^{N} \frac{C}{(1+r)^N} + \frac{M}{(1+r)^N}
\end{aligned} \tag{2.1}$$

where
    P is the price
    C is the annual coupon payment

r is the discount rate (therefore, the required yield)

N is the number of years to maturity (therefore, the number of interest periods in an annually-paying bond; for a semi-annual bond the number of interest periods is $N \times 2$)

M is the maturity payment or par value (usually 100 per cent of currency).

For long-hand calculation purposes the first half of (2.1) is usually simplified and in fact can be expressed in two ways as shown by (2.2) below.

$$P = C \frac{1 - \left[\frac{1}{(1+r)^N}\right]}{r}$$

or

$$P = \frac{C}{r}\left[1 - \frac{1}{(1+r)^N}\right] \tag{2.2}$$

The price of a bond that pays semi-annual coupons is given by the expression at (2.3), which is our earlier expression modified to allow for the twice-yearly discounting:

$$
\begin{aligned}
P &= \frac{\frac{C}{2}}{\left(1+\frac{1}{2}r\right)} + \frac{\frac{C}{2}}{\left(1+\frac{1}{2}r\right)^2} + \frac{\frac{C}{2}}{\left(1+\frac{1}{2}r\right)^3} + \cdots\cdots + \frac{\frac{C}{2}}{\left(1+\frac{1}{2}r\right)^{2N}} + \frac{M}{\left(1+\frac{1}{2}r\right)^{2N}} \\
&= \sum_{t=1}^{2T} \frac{\frac{C}{2}}{\left(1+\frac{1}{2}r\right)^N} + \frac{M}{\left(1+\frac{1}{2}r\right)^{2N}} \\
&= \frac{C}{r}\left[1 - \frac{1}{\left(1+\frac{1}{2}r\right)^{2N}}\right] + \frac{M}{\left(1+\frac{1}{2}r\right)^{2N}}
\end{aligned}
\tag{2.3}
$$

Note how we set $2N$ as the power to which to raise the discount factor, as there are two interest payments every year for a bond that pays semi-annually. Therefore a more convenient function to use might be the number of interest periods in the life of the bond, as opposed to the number of years to maturity, which we could set as n, allowing us to alter the equation for a semi-annually paying bond as:

$$P = \frac{C}{r}\left[1 - \frac{1}{\left(1+\frac{1}{2}r\right)^n}\right] + \frac{M}{\left(1+\frac{1}{2}r\right)^n} \tag{2.4}$$

The formula at (2.4) calculates the fair price on a coupon payment date, so that there is no *accrued interest* incorporated into the price. It also assumes that there is an even number of coupon payment dates remaining before maturity.

The date used as the point for calculation is the *settlement date* for the bond, the date on which a bond will change hands after it is traded. For a new issue of bonds the settlement date is the day when the stock is delivered to investors and payment is received by the bond issuer. The settlement date for a bond traded in the *secondary market* is the day that the buyer transfers payment to the seller of the bond and when the seller transfers the bond to the buyer. Different markets will have different settlement conventions, for example UK gilts normally settle one business day after the trade date (the notation used in bond markets is "$T+1$") whereas Eurobonds settle on $T+3$. The term *value date* is sometimes used in place of settlement date, however the two terms are not strictly synonymous. A settlement date can only fall on a business date, so that a gilt traded on a Friday will settle on a Monday. However a value date can sometimes fall on a non-business day, for example when accrued interest is being calculated.

The standard price formula also assumes that the bond is traded for price settlement on a day that is precisely one interest period before the next coupon payment. The price formula is adjusted if dealing takes place between coupon dates. If we take the value date (almost always the settlement date, although unlike the settlement date the value date can fall on a non-working day) for any transaction, we then need to calculate the number of calendar days from this day to the next coupon date. We then use the following ratio i when adjusting the exponent for the discount factor:

$$i = \frac{\text{Days from value date to next coupon date}}{\text{Days in the interest period}}$$

The number of days in the interest period is the number of calendar days between the last coupon date and the next one, and it will depend on the day count basis used for that specific bond; this is covered in the section on day counts. The price formula is then modified as shown at (2.5),

$$P = \frac{C}{(1+r)^i} + \frac{C}{(1+r)^{1+i}} + \frac{C}{(1+r)^{2+i}} + \cdots\cdots + \frac{C}{(1+r)^{n-1+i}}$$
$$+ \frac{M}{(1+r)^{n-1+i}} \tag{2.5}$$

where the variables C, M, n and r are as before. Note that (2.5) assumes r for an annually-paying bond and is adjusted to $r/2$ for a semi-annually paying bond.

Example 2.1
In these examples we illustrate the long-hand price calculation, using both expressions for the calculation of the present value of the annuity stream of a bond's cash flows.

2.1(a)
Calculate the fair pricing of a UK gilt, the 9% Treasury 2008, which pays semi-annual coupons, with the following terms:
$C = £9.00$ per £100 nominal
$M = £100$
$N = 10$ years (that is, the calculation is for value on 13 October 1998)
$r = 4.98\%$

$$P = \frac{9.00}{0.0498}\left[1 - \frac{1}{\left[1 + \frac{1}{2}(0.0498)\right]^{20}}\right] + \frac{100}{\left[1 + \frac{1}{2}(0.0498)\right]^{20}}$$
$$= 70.2175 + 61.1463$$
$$= 131.3638$$

The fair price of the gilt is £131.3638, which is composed of the present value of the stream of coupon payments (£70.2175) and the present value of the return of the principal (£61.1463).

2.1(b)
What is the price of a 5% coupon sterling bond with precisely 5 years to maturity, with semi-annual coupon payments, if the yield required is 5.40%?

As the cash flows for this bond are 10 semi-annual coupons of £2.50 and a redemption payment of £100 in 10 six-month periods from now, the price of the bond can be obtained by solving the following expression, where we substitute $C = 2.5$, $n = 10$ and $r = 0.027$ into the price equation (the values for C and r reflect the adjustments necessary for a semi-annual paying bond).

$$P = 2.5\left[\frac{1 - \left[\frac{1}{(1.027)^{10}}\right]}{0.027}\right] + \frac{100}{(1.027)^{10}}$$
$$= 21.65574 + 76.61178$$
$$= 98.26752$$

The price of the bond is £98.2675 per £100 nominal.

2.1(c)
What is the price of a 5% coupon euro bond with five years to maturity paying annual coupons, again with a required yield of 5.40%?

In this case there are five periods of interest, so we may set $C = 5$, $n = 5$, with $r = 0.05$.

$$P = 5\left[\frac{1 - \left[\frac{1}{(1.054)^{5}}\right]}{0.054}\right] + \frac{100}{(1.054)^{5}}$$
$$= 21.410121 + 76.877092$$
$$= 98.287213$$

Note how the annual-paying bond has a slightly higher price for the same required annualised yield. This is because the semi-annual paying sterling bond has a higher effective yield than the euro bond, resulting in a lower price.

2.1(d)

Consider our 5% sterling bond again, but this time the required yield has risen and is now 6%. This makes $C=2.5$, $n=10$ and $r=0.03$.

$$P = 2.5 \left[\frac{1 - \left[\frac{1}{(1.03)^{10}} \right]}{0.03} \right] + \frac{100}{(1.03)^{10}}$$

$$= 21.325507 + 74.409391$$

$$= 95.734898$$

As the required yield has risen, the discount rate used in the price calculation is now higher, and the result of the higher discount is a lower present value (price).

2.1(e)

Calculate the price of our sterling bond, still with five years to maturity but offering a yield of 5.10%.

$$P = 2.5 \left[\frac{1 - \left[\frac{1}{(1.0255)^{10}} \right]}{0.0255} \right] + \frac{100}{(1.0255)^{10}}$$

$$= 21.823737 + 77.739788$$

$$= 99.563525$$

To satisfy the lower required yield of 5.10% the price of the bond has fallen to £99.56 per £100.

2.1(f)

Calculate the price of the 5% sterling bond one year later, with precisely four years left to maturity and with the required yield still at the original 5.40%. This sets the terms in 2.1(a) unchanged, except now $n=8$.

$$P = 2.5 \left[\frac{1 - \left[\frac{1}{(1.027)^{8}} \right]}{0.027} \right] + \frac{100}{(1.027)^{8}}$$

$$= 17.773458 + 80.804668$$

$$= 98.578126$$

The price of the bond is £98.58. Compared to 2.1(b) this illustrates how, other things being equal, the price of a bond will approach par (£100 per cent) as it approaches maturity.

2.5.4 Pricing undated bonds

There also exist *perpetual* or *irredeemable* bonds which have no redemption date, so that interest on them is paid indefinitely. They are also known as *undated* bonds. An example of an undated bond is the $3\frac{1}{2}\%$ War Loan, a gilt formed out of issues in 1916 to help pay for the 1914–1918 war effort. Most undated bonds date from a long time in the past and it is unusual to see them issued today. In structure the cash flow from an undated bond can be viewed as a continuous annuity. The fair price of such a bond is given from (2.1) by setting $N = \infty$, such that:

$$P = \frac{C}{r} \tag{2.6}$$

where the inputs C and r are as before.

2.5.5 Bond price quotations

The convention in most bond markets is to quote prices as a percentage of par. The value of par is assumed to be 100 units of currency unless otherwise stated. A sterling bond quoted at an *offer* price of £98.45 means that £100 nominal of the bond will cost a buyer £98.45. A bond selling at below par is considered to be trading at a *discount*, while a price above par means the bond is trading at a *premium* to par. Do not confuse the term trading at a discount with a discount instrument however, which generally refers to a zero-coupon bond.

In most markets bond prices are quoted in decimals, in minimum increments of 1/100ths. This is the case for example with Eurobonds, euro denominated bonds and gilts. Certain markets including the US Treasury market for example, and certain Commonwealth country markets such as South African and Indian government bonds quote prices in *ticks*, where the minimum increment is 1/32nd One tick is therefore equal to 0.03125. A US Treasury might be priced at "98–05" which means "98 and 5 ticks". This is equal to 98 and 5/32nds which is 98.15625.

Example 2.2

■ What is the total consideration for £5 million nominal of a gilt, where the price is 114.50?
The price of the gilt is £114.50 per £100, so the consideration is:

$$1.145 \times 5,000,000 = 5,725,000$$

■ What consideration is payable for $5 million nominal of a US Treasury, quoted at an all-in price of 99–16?

The US Treasury price is 99–16, which is equal to 99 and 16/32, or 99.50 per $100. The consideration is therefore:

$$0.9950 \times 5,000,000 = \$4,975,000$$

If the price of a bond is below par the total consideration is below the nominal amount, whereas if it is priced above par the consideration will be above the nominal amount.

2.6   Clean and dirty bond prices

2.6.1 Accrued interest

Our discussion of bond pricing up to now has ignored coupon interest. All bonds (except zero-coupon bonds) accrue interest on a daily basis, and this is then paid out on the coupon date. The calculation of bond prices using present value analysis does not account for coupon interest or *accrued interest*. In all major bond markets the convention is to quote price as a *clean price*. This is the price of the bond as given by the net present value of its cash flows, but excluding coupon interest that has accrued on the bond since the last dividend payment. As all bonds accrue interest on a daily basis, even if a bond is held for only one day, interest will have been earned by the bondholder. However we have referred already to a bond's *all-in* price, which is the price that is actually paid for the bond in the market. This is also known as the *dirty price* (or *gross price*), which is the clean price of a bond plus accrued interest. In other words the accrued interest must be added to the quoted price to get the total consideration for the bond.

Accruing interest compensates the seller of the bond for giving up all of the next coupon payment even though they will have held the bond for part of the period since the last coupon payment. The clean price for a bond will move with changes in market interest rates; assuming that this is constant in a coupon period, the clean price will be constant for this period. However the dirty price for the same bond will increase steadily from one interest payment date until the next one. On the coupon date the clean and dirty prices are the same and the accrued interest is zero. Between the coupon payment date and the next *ex-dividend* date the bond is traded *cum dividend*, so that the buyer gets the next coupon payment. The seller is compensated for not receiving the next coupon payment by receiving accrued interest instead. This is positive and increases up to the next ex-dividend date, at which point the dirty price falls by the present value of the amount of the coupon payment. The dirty price at this point is below the clean price, reflecting the fact that accrued interest is now negative. This is because after the ex-dividend date the bond is traded "ex-dividend"; the seller not the buyer receives the next coupon and the buyer has to be compensated for not receiving the next coupon by means of a lower price for holding the bond.

The net interest accrued since the last ex-dividend date is determined as follows:

$$AI = C \times \left[\frac{N_{xt} - N_{xc}}{\text{Day Base}} \right] \qquad (2.7)$$

where

AI	is the next accrued interest
C	is the bond coupon
N_{xc}	is the number of days between the ex-dividend date and the coupon payment date (7 business days for UK gilts)
N_{xt}	is the number of days between the ex-dividend date and the date for the calculation
Day Base	is the day count base (usually 365 or 360).

Interest accrues on a bond from and including the last coupon date up to and excluding what is called the *value date*. The value date is almost always the *settlement* date for the bond, or the date when a bond is passed to the buyer and the seller receives payment. Interest does not accrue on bonds whose issuer has subsequently gone into default. Bonds that trade without accrued interest are said to be trading *flat* or *clean*. By definition therefore,

Clean price of a bond = Dirty price − AI.

For bonds that are trading ex-dividend, the accrued coupon is negative and would be subtracted from the clean price. The calculation is given by (2.8) below.

$$AI = -C \times \frac{\text{Days to next coupon}}{\text{Day Base}} \tag{2.8}$$

Certain classes of bonds, for example US Treasuries and Eurobonds, do not have an ex-dividend period and therefore trade cum dividend right up to the coupon date.

2.6.2 Accrual day count conventions

The accrued interest calculation for a bond is dependent on the day-count basis specified for the bond in question. We have already seen that when bonds are traded in the market the actual consideration that changes hands is made up of the clean price of the bond together with the accrued that has accumulated on the bond since the last coupon payment; these two components make up the dirty price of the bond. When calculating the accrued interest, the market will use the appropriate day-count convention for that bond. A particular market will apply one of five different methods to calculate accrued interest; these are:

actual/365	Accrued = Coupon × days/365
actual/360	Accrued = Coupon × days/360
actual/actual	Accrued = Coupon × days/actual number of days in the interest period
30/360	See below
30E/360	See below

Market	Coupon frequency	Day count basis	Ex-dividend period
Australia	Semi-annual	actual/actual	Yes
Austria	Annual	actual/actual	No
Belgium	Annual	actual/actual	No
Canada	Semi-annual	actual/actual	No
Denmark	Annual	actual/actual	Yes
Eurobonds	Annual	30/360	No
France	Annual	actual/actual	No
Germany	Annual	actual/actual	No
Eire	Annual	actual/actual	No
Italy	Annual	actual/actual	No
New Zealand	Semi-annual	actual/actual	Yes
Norway	Annual	actual/365	Yes
Spain	Annual	actual/actual	No
Sweden	Annual	30E/360	Yes
Switzerland	Annual	30E/360	No
United Kingdom	Semi-annual	actual/actual	Yes
United States	Semi-annual	actual/actual	No

Table 2.2: Government bond market accrued interest conventions.

When determining the number of days in between two dates, include the first date but not the second; thus, under the actual/365 convention, there are 37 days between 4 August and 10 September. The last two conventions assume 30 days in each month, so for example there are "30 days" between 10 February and 10 March. Under the 30/360 convention, if the first date falls on the 31st, it is changed to the 30th of the month, and if the second date falls on the 31st and the first date is on the 30th or 31st, the second date is changed to the 30th. The difference under the 30E/360 method is that if the second date falls on the 31st of the month it is automatically changed to the 30th.

The day count basis, together with the coupon frequency, of selected major government bond markets around the world is given in Table 2.2.

Example 2.3 Accrual calculation for 7% Treasury 2002
This gilt has coupon dates of 7 June and 7 December each year. £100 nominal of the bond is traded for value on 27 August 1998. What is the accrued interest on the value date?

On the value date 81 days have passed since the last coupon date. Under the old system for gilts, act/365, the calculation was:

$$7 \times \frac{81}{365} = 1.55342.$$

Under the current system of act/act, which came into effect for gilts in

November 1998, the accrued calculation uses the actual number of days between the two coupon dates, giving us:

$$7 \times \frac{81}{183} \times 0.5 = 1.54918$$

Example 2.4

Mansur buys £25,000 nominal of the 7% 2002 gilt for value on 27 August 1998, at a price of 102.4375. How much does he actually pay for the bond? The clean price of the bond is 102.4375. The dirty price of the bond is:

$$102.4375 + 1.55342 = 103.99092$$

The total consideration is therefore 1.0399092 × 25,000 = £25,997.73.

Example 2.5

A Norwegian government bond with a coupon of 8% is purchased for settlement on 30 July 1999 at a price of 99.50. Assume that this is 7 days before the coupon date and therefore the bond trades ex-dividend. What is the all-in price?

$$\text{The accrued interest} = -8 \times \frac{7}{365} = -0.153424$$

The all-in price is therefore $99.50 - 0.1534 = 99.3466$

2.7 Market yield

We referred in Section 2.5.2 to the yield that is "required" by the market at any one time. Just as there are many different types of bond and many different types of borrower, so there are different types of yield. The price of any bond will change in line with changes in required yield, so that straight away we can see that it is not price changes that we are really interested in, but yields. It is a change in required yield that will drive a change in price1.[1] So in the bond market we are concerned with examining the determinants of market yields.

The main quoted yield in any market is the government bond yield. This is the yield on a domestic market's government bonds. The required yield on these bonds is mainly a function of the central bank's *base rate* or *minimum lending rate*, set by the government or central bank. Other factors will also impact the

---

[1] We have observed how the price of a bond will gradually converge towards par as it approaches maturity, irrespective of the price it trades at during its life. However this is an automatic process and a mechanical price change that is part of the properties of a bond. As such it need not concern us unduly.

yield, including the relative size of the public sector budget deficit and national debt as a percentage of the national product (usually measured as Gross Domestic Product or Gross National Product), the economic policies that are adopted, and of course supply and demand for government bonds themselves. A change in any of these factors can and does affect government bond prices. While it is common to view government bonds as the safest credit for investors, this really only applies to the largest developed country markets. Certain countries within the Organisation for Economic Co-operation and Development (OECD), for example, Greece, South Korea and Mexico, do not have their government debt given the highest possible rating by credit analysts.

Bonds issued by non-sovereign borrowers will be priced off government bonds, which means that the yields required on them will be at some level above their respective government bond yields, if they are domestic currency bonds. Bond yields are often quoted as a *yield spread* over the equivalent government bond. This is known as the *credit spread* on a bond. A change in the required credit spread for any bond will affect the bond's price. Credit spreads will fluctuate for a variety of reasons, including when there is a change in the way the borrower is perceived in the market (such as a poor set of financial results by a corporate), which will affect the rate at which the borrower can raise funds. Credit spreads can sometimes change because comparable bonds yields change, as well as due to supply and demand factors and liquidity factors.

2.7.1 Yield measurement

Bonds are generally traded on the basis of their prices but because of the complicated patterns of cash flows that different bonds can have, they are generally compared in terms of their yields. This means that a market-maker will usually quote a two-way price at which they will buy or sell a particular bond, but it is the yield at which the bond is trading that is important to the market-maker's customer. This is because a bond's price does not actually tell us anything useful about what we are getting. Remember that in any market there will be a number of bonds with different issuers, coupons and terms to maturity. Even in a homogenous market such as the gilt market, different gilts will trade according to their own specific characteristics. To compare bonds in the market therefore we need the yield on any bond and it is yields that we compare, not prices. A fund manager quoted a price at which they can buy a bond will be instantly aware of what yield that price represents, and whether this yield represents fair value. So it is the yield represented by the price that is the important figure for bond traders.

The yield on any investment is the interest rate that will make the present value of the cash flows from the investment equal to the initial cost (price) of the investment. So mathematically the yield on any investment is the interest rate that satisfies our basic bond price equation introduced earlier as equation (2.1).

But as we have noted there are other types of yield measure used in the market for different purposes. The most important of these are bond redemption yields, *spot* rates and *forward* rates. We will now discuss each type of yield measure and show how it is computed, followed by a discussion of the relative usefulness of each measure.

2.7.2 Current yield

The simplest measure of the yield on a bond is the *current yield*, also known as the *flat yield, interest yield* or *running yield*. The running yield is given by (2.9).

$$rc = \frac{C}{P} \times 100 \qquad (2.9)$$

where

  rc is the current yield
  C is the bond coupon
  P is the clean price of the bond.

In (2.9) C is not expressed as a decimal. Current yield ignores any capital gain or loss that might arise from holding and trading a bond and does not consider the time value of money. It essentially calculates the bond coupon income as a proportion of the price paid for the bond, and to be accurate would have to assume that the bond was more like an annuity rather than a fixed-term instrument.

The current yield is useful as a "rough-and-ready" interest rate calculation; it is often used to estimate the cost of or profit from a short-term holding of a bond. For example if other short-term interest rates such as the one-week or three-month rates are higher than the current yield, holding the bond is said to involve a *running cost*. This is also known as *negative carry* or *negative funding*. The term is used by bond traders and market makers and *leveraged* investors. The *carry* on a bond is a useful measure for all market practitioners as it illustrates the cost of holding or funding a bond. The funding rate is the bondholder's short-term cost of funds. A private investor could also apply this to a short-term holding of bonds.

Example 2.6   Running yield
A bond with a coupon of 6% is trading at a clean price of 97.89. What is the current yield of the bond?

$$rc = \frac{6.00}{97.89} \times 100$$
$$= 6.129\%$$

Example 2.7

What is the current yield of a bond with 7% coupon and a clean price of 103.49?

$$rc = \frac{7}{103.49} \times 100$$
$$= 6.76\%$$

Note from examples 2.6 and 2.7 that the current yield of a bond will lie above the coupon rate if the price of the bond is below par, and vice-versa if the price is above par.

2.7.3 Yield to maturity

The *yield to maturity* (YTM) or *gross redemption yield* is the most frequently used measure of return from holding a bond.[2] Yield to maturity takes into account the pattern of coupon payments, the bond's term to maturity and the capital gain (or loss) arising over the remaining life of the bond. We saw from our bond price in equation (2.1) that these elements were all related and were important components determining a bond's price. If we set the IRR for a set of cash flows to be the rate that applies from a start date to an end date we can assume the IRR to be the YTM for those cash flows. The YTM therefore is equivalent to the *internal rate of return* (IRR) on the bond, the rate that equates the value of the discounted cash flows on the bond to its current price. The calculation assumes that the bond is held until maturity and therefore it is the cash flows to maturity that are discounted in the calculation. It also employs the concept of the time value of money.

As we would expect the formula for YTM is essentially that for calculating the price of a bond. For a bond paying annual coupons the YTM is calculated by solving equation (2.10), and we assume that the first coupon will be paid exactly one interest period from now (which, for an annual coupon bond is exactly one year from now).

$$P_d = \frac{C}{(1 + rm)^1} + \frac{C}{(1 + rm)^2} + \frac{C}{(1 + rm)^3} + \cdots\cdots + \frac{C}{(1 + rm)^n}$$
$$+ \frac{M}{(1 + rm)^n} \tag{2.10}$$

where

---

[2] In this book the terms *yield to maturity* and *gross redemption yield* are used synonymously. The latter term is encountered in sterling markets.

Pd is the bond dirty price
C is the coupon rate
M is the par or redemption payment (100)
Rm is the annual yield to maturity (the YTM)
N is the number of interest periods.

Note that the number of interest periods in an annual-coupon bond is equal to the number of years to maturity, and so for these bonds n is equal to the number of years to maturity.

We can simplify (2.10) using Σ where "Σ" means "is the sum of".

$$P_d = \sum_{n=1}^{N} \frac{C}{(1+rm)^n} + \frac{M}{(1+rm)^n} \qquad (2.11)$$

Note that the expression at (2.11) has two variable parameters, the price Pd and yield rm. It cannot be re-arranged to solve for yield rm explicitly and in fact the only way to solve for the yield is to use the process of numerical iteration. The process involves estimating a value for rm and calculating the price associated with the estimated yield. If the calculated price is higher than the price of the bond at the time, the yield estimate is lower than the actual yield, and so it must be adjusted until it converges to the level that corresponds with the bond price.[3] For YTM for a semi-annual coupon bond we have to adjust the formula to allow for the semi-annual payments. Equation (2.11) is modified as shown by (2.12), again assuming there are precisely six months to the next coupon payment.

$$P_d = \sum_{n=1}^{N} \frac{\frac{C}{2}}{\left(1+\frac{1}{2}rm\right)^n} + \frac{M}{\left(1+\frac{1}{2}rm\right)^n} \qquad (2.12)$$

where n is now the number of interest periods in the life of the bond and therefore equal to the number of years to maturity multiplied by 2.

All the YTM equations above use rm to discount a bond's cash flows back to the next coupon payment and then discount the value at that date back to the date of the calculation. In other words rm is the internal rate of return that equates the value of the discounted cash flows on the bond to the current dirty price of the bond (at the current date). The internal rate of return is the discount rate which, if applied to all of the cash flows will solve for a number that is equal to the dirty price of the bond (its present value). By assuming that this rate will be unchanged for the reinvestment of all the coupon cash flows, and that the instrument will be held to maturity, the IRR can then be seen as the yield to maturity. In effect both measures are identical; the assumption of uniform reinvestment rate allows us to calculate

---

[3] The Bloomberg also uses the term yield-to-workout where "workout" refers to the maturity date for the bond.

the IRR as equivalent to the redemption yield. It is common for the IRR measure to be used by corporate financiers for project appraisal, while the redemption yield measure is used in bond markets. The solution to the equation for rm cannot be found analytically and has to be solved through numerical iteration, that is, by estimating the yield from two trial values for rm, then solving by using the formula for linear interpolation. It is more common nowadays to use a spreadsheet programme or programmable calculator such as a Hewlett-Packard calculator.

Note that the redemption yield as discussed in this section is the gross redemption yield, the yield that results from payment of coupons without deduction of any withholding tax. The *net redemption yield* is obtained by multiplying the coupon rate C by (1 – marginal tax rate). The net yield is what will be received if the bond is traded in a market where bonds pay coupon net, which means net of a withholding tax. The net redemption yield is always lower than the gross redemption yield.

2.7.4 Using the redemption yield calculation

We have already alluded to the key assumption behind the YTM calculation, namely that the rate rm remains stable for the entire period of the life of the bond. By assuming the same yield we can say that all coupons are reinvested at the same yield rm. For the bond in example 2.8 this means that if all the cash flows are discounted at 6.5% they will have a total present value or NPV of 97.89. At the same time if all the cash flows received during the life of the bond are reinvested at 6.5% until the maturity of the bond, the final redemption yield will be 6.5%. This is patently unrealistic since we can predict with virtual certainty that interest rates for instruments of similar maturity to the bond at each coupon date will not remain at 6.5% for five years.

In practice, however, investors require a rate of return that is equivalent to the price that they are paying for a bond and the redemption yield is, to put it simply, as good a measurement as any. A more accurate measurement might be to calculate present values of future cash flows using the discount rate that is equal to the market's view on where interest rates will be at that point, known as the *forward* interest rate. However forward rates are *implied* interest rates, and a YTM measurement calculated using forward rates can be as speculative as one calculated using the conventional formula. This is because the actual market interest rate at any time is invariably different from the rate implied earlier in the forward markets. So a YTM calculation made using forward rates would not be realised in practice either.[4] We shall see later in this chapter how the *zero-coupon* interest rate is the true interest rate for any term to maturity. However the YTM is, despite the limitations presented by its assumptions, the main measure of return used in the markets.

---

[4] Such an approach is used to price interest-rate swaps, however.

> **Example 2.8   Comparing the different yield measures**
> The examples in this section illustrated a five-year bond with a coupon of 6%
> trading at a price of 97.89. Using the three common measures of return we
> have:
>
> | | |
> |---|---|
> | Running yield | $= 6.129\%$ |
> | Simple yield | $= 6.560\%$ |
> | Redemption yield | $= 6.50\%$ |

2.8   Bond pricing and yield

The approach we have described is very much the traditional one. Academic texts
express bond prices and yields in different terms, which we consider briefly now.
The terminology is that used in leading texts including Jarrow (1996), Neftci
(1996), Baxter and Rennie (1996) and Hull (1997).

Consider a zero-coupon bond that has a maturity date at time T. The price of
this bond today (at time t) is denoted by $P(t, T)$ and given by (2.13) below,

$$P(t, T) = \frac{1}{[r(t, T)]^{(T-t)}} \tag{2.13}$$

where $r(t, T)$ is the yield of the T-maturity bond at time t. Expression (2.13) above
can be re-written as follows, in terms of the bond yield.

$$r(t, T) = \left[\frac{1}{P(t, T)}\right]^{1/(T, t)} \tag{2.14}$$

This states that the yield on the zero-coupon bond is the percentage return earned
in the period from the time the bond is held (t) to its maturity date T.

We can then derive an expression for the bond price in terms of a *forward rate*.
The forward rate $rf(t, T)$ is the rate that applies at time t for the period $(T, T+1)$
and is given by (2.15) below,

$$rf(t, T) = \frac{P(t, T)}{P(t, T + 1)} \tag{2.15}$$

and is the interest-rate that is earned on a deposit over the time period $(T, T+1)$
that has been put on at time t. Expression (2.1) above may be used to obtain a
formula for the price of a bond, given below.

$$P(T, t) = \frac{1}{\prod_{j=t}^{T-1} rf(t, j)} \tag{2.16}$$

Expression (2.16) states the price of a bond in terms of the forward rates for
maturity periods up to the maturity of the bond itself. For a zero-coupon bond the

price is the present value of 1 that is received at time T, discounted at the forward rates that apply to each interest period from t to the maturity date. This is the bond price expression found in later texts. In fact the bond price is usually given in terms of an *integral* of forward rates, because rates are analysed as occurring in a *continuous time* environment. This is an advanced area of bond mathematics and interested readers should consult the texts listed in the bibliography. The derivation of (2.16) is given in Jarrow (1996) and other texts.

2.9 The price/yield relationship

This chapter has illustrated a fundamental property of bonds, namely that an upward change in the price results in a downward move in the yield, and vice-versa. This is of course immediately apparent since the price is the present value of the cash flows; as the required yield for a bond say decreases, the present value and hence the price of the cash flow for the bond will increase. It also reflects the fact that for plain vanilla bonds the coupon is fixed, therefore it is the price of the bond that will need to fluctuate to reflect changes in market yields. It is useful sometimes to plot the relationship between yield and price for a bond. A typical price/yield profile is represented graphically at Figure 2.2, which shows a *convex* curve.

To reiterate, for a plain vanilla bond with a fixed coupon, the price is the only variable that can change to reflect changes in the market environment. When the coupon rate of a bond is equal to the market rate, the bond price will be par (100). If the required interest rate in the market moves above a bond's coupon rate at any

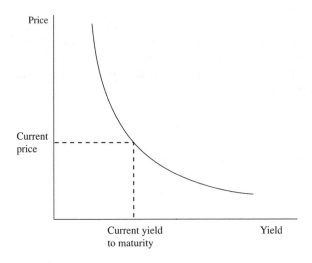

Figure 2.2: The bond price/yield relationship.

point in time, the price of the bond will adjust downward in order for the bondholder to realise the additional return required. Similarly if the required yield moves below the coupon rate, the price will move up to equate the yield on the bond to the market rate. As a bond will redeem at par, the capital appreciation realised on maturity acts as compensation when the coupon rate is lower than the market yield.

The price of a bond will move for a variety of reasons, including the market-related ones noted here:

■ when there is a change in the yield required by the market, either because of changes in the base rate or a perceived change in credit quality of the bond issuer (credit considerations do not affect developed country government bonds);
■ when there is a change because as the bond is approaching maturity, its price moves gradually towards par;
■ when there is a change in the market-required yield due to a change in the yield on comparable bonds.

Bond prices also move for liquidity reasons and normal supply-and-demand reasons, for example if there is a large amount of a particular bond in issue it is easier to trade the bond; also if there is demand due to a large customer base for the bond. Liquidity is a general term used here to mean the ease with which a market participant can trade in or out of a position. If there is always a ready buyer or seller for a particular bond, it will be easier to trade in the market.

Table 2.3 shows the prices for a hypothetical 7% coupon, quoted for settlement on 10 August 1999 and maturing on 10 August 2004. The bond pays annual coupons on a 30/360 basis. The prices are calculated by inserting the required

Yield (%)	Price
4.0	113.3555
4.5	110.9750
5.0	108.6590
5.5	106.4054
6.0	104.2124
6.5	102.0778
7.0	**100.0000**
7.5	97.9770
8.0	96.0073
8.5	94.0890
9.0	92.2207
9.5	90.4007
10.0	88.6276

Table 2.3: Prices and yields for a 7% five-year bond.

yield values into the standard formulae for a set of cash flows. We can calculate the present value of the annuity stream represented by the bond and the present value of the final maturity payment. Note that when the required yield is at the same level as the bond's fixed coupon (in this case 7%) the price of the bond is 100 per cent, or *par*.

2.9.1 Coupon, yield and price relationship

The bond markets are also known as the "fixed income" or "fixed interest" markets. This reflects the fact that the coupon for conventional bonds is fixed, and in most cases the maturity date is also fixed. Therefore when required yield levels in the market change, the price is the only factor that can change to reflect the new market yield levels. We saw in Table 2.3 how the price of our hypothetical 7% five-year bond changed as the required yield changed. This is an important result. Let us consider the situation – if the required yield in the market for our 7% bond is fixed, investors will be happy to hold the bond. What if required yields subsequently rise above the 7% level? Bondholders will be unhappy as they are now being paid 7% when elsewhere in the market higher yields are available. The market price of the bond will therefore change so that the yield on the bond changes, to compensate bondholders. If the required yield for the bond changes to 8%, we see from Table 2.3 that the price has fallen from par to 96.00. If this did not happen bondholders would sell the 7% issue and buy a bond that was yielding 8%; the market price mechanism ensures that this does not happen. If the situation is reversed the price mechanism will again operate to equalise the yield on the bond with those prevalent in the marketplace. If required yields drop to 6% the bond price rises to 104.21, because bondholders would now be receiving 7% when yields available in the market are now only 6%. We can see then that when required yield in the market is equal to a bond's coupon, the bond price will be par; the price will move respectively above or below par if required yields are below or above the coupon rate.

If a bond is priced at below its par value it is said to be trading at a *discount*, while if it is trading above par value it is said to be trading at a *premium* to its par value.

When merchant banks issue bonds on behalf of borrowers, they will set a bond's coupon at the level that would make the bond price equal to par. This means that the bond coupon will be equal to the yield required by the market at the time of issue. The bond's price would then fluctuate as market yields changed, as we showed in Table 2.3. Investors generally prefer to pay par or just under par when they buy a new issue of bonds, which is why a merchant bank will set the coupon that equates the bond price to par or in a range between 99.00 and par. The reason behind this preference to pay no more than par is often purely cosmetic, since an issue price above par would simply indicate a coupon higher than the market rate.

However, as many fund managers and investors buy a bond and hold it until maturity, one often finds this prejudice against paying over par for a new issue.

What will happen if market yields remain unchanged during the life of a bond from when it was issued? In this unlikely scenario the price of a conventional bond will remain unchanged at par. The price of any bond will ultimately equal its redemption value, which is par. Therefore a bond that is priced at a premium or a discount will gradually converge to par as it approaches maturity.

As a bond approaches maturity there are fewer and fewer coupon payments, so that progressively more of the bond's price is made up of the present value of the final redemption payment. The present value of this payment will steadily increase as the maturity date is approached, since it is being discounted over a shorter period of time. The present value of the annuity cash flows of the bond steadily declines as we get fewer of them, and this is not offset by the increase in value of the maturity payment. Hence the price of the bond steadily declines. The opposite happens when the bond price starts off at a discount, where the increase in the value of the maturity payment outweighs the decrease in the price of the coupons, so that the bond price steadily converges to par.

Example 2.9

Illustration of price/yield changes for two selected gilts

Prices of selected gilts on 14 July 1999 for next-day settlement

UK Treasury stock 5% 2004

Price	Yield %
98.61750	5.324
98.64875	5.317
98.68000	5.309 (actual quoted price at the time of asking)
98.71100	5.302
98.74200	5.295

UK Treasury stock 5 $\frac{3}{4}$% 2009

Price	Yield %
104.73750	5.155
104.76875	5.151
104.80000	5.147 (actual quoted price at the time of asking)
104.83125	5.143
104.86250	5.140

2.10 Duration, modified duration and convexity

Bonds pay a part of their total return during their lifetime, in the form of coupon interest, so that the term to maturity does not reflect the true period over which the bond's return is earned. Additionally if we wish to gain an idea of the trading characteristics of a bond, and compare this to other bonds of say, similar maturity, term to maturity is insufficient and so we need a more accurate measure. A plain vanilla coupon bond pays out a proportion of its return during the course of its life, in the form of coupon interest. If we were to analyse the properties of a bond, we should conclude quite quickly that its maturity gives us little indication of how much of its return is paid out during its life, nor any idea of the timing or size of its cash flows, and hence its sensitivity to moves in market interest rates. For example, if comparing two bonds with the same maturity date but different coupons, the higher coupon bond provides a larger proportion of its return in the form of coupon income than does the lower coupon bond. The higher coupon bond provides its return at a faster rate; its value is theoretically therefore less subject to subsequent fluctuations in interest rates.

We may wish to calculate an average of the time to receipt of a bond's cash flows, and use this measure as a more realistic indication of maturity. However, cash flows during the life of a bond are not all equal in value, so a more accurate measure would be to take the average time to receipt of a bond's cash flows, but weighted in the form of the cash flows' present value. This is, in effect, *duration*. We can measure the speed of payment of a bond, and hence its price risk relative to other bonds of the same maturity by measuring the average maturity of the bond's cash flow stream. Bond analysts use duration to measure this property (it is sometimes known as *Macaulay's duration*, after its inventor, who first introduced it in 1938).[5] Duration is the weighted average time until the receipt of cash flows from a bond, where the weights are the present values of the cash flows, measured in years. At the time that he introduced the concept, Macaulay used the duration measure as an alternative for the length of time that a bond investment had remaining to maturity.

2.10.1 Duration

Recall that the price/yield formula for a plain vanilla bond is as given at (2.17) below, assuming complete years to maturity paying annual coupons, and with no accrued interest at the calculation date. The yield to maturity reverts to the symbol r in this section.

$$P = \frac{C}{(1+r)} + \frac{C}{(1+r)^2} + \frac{C}{(1+r)^3} + \cdots\cdots + \frac{C}{(1+r)^n} + \frac{M}{(1+r)^n} \qquad (2.17)$$

---

[5] Macaulay, F., *Some theoretical problems suggested by the movements of interest rates, bond yields and stock prices in the United States since 1865*, National Bureau of Economic Research, NY 1938. This remains a fascinating read and is available from Risk Classics publishing, under the title *Interest rates, bond yields and stock prices in the United States since 1856*.

If we take the first derivative of this expression we obtain (2.18).

$$\frac{dP}{dr} = \frac{-1C}{(1+r)^2} + \frac{-2C}{(1+r)^3} + \cdots\cdots + \frac{(-n)C}{(1+r)^{n+1}} + \frac{(-n)M}{(1+r)^{n+1}} \tag{2.18}$$

If we re-arrange (2.18) we will obtain the expression at (2.19), which is our equation to calculate the approximate change in price for a small change in yield.

$$\frac{dP}{dr} = -\frac{1}{(1+r)} \left[\frac{1C}{(1+r)} + \frac{2C}{(1+r)^2} + \cdots\cdots + \frac{nC}{(1+r)^n} + \frac{nM}{(1+r)^n} \right] \tag{2.19}$$

Readers may feel a sense of familiarity regarding the expression in brackets in equation (2.19) as this is the weighted average time to maturity of the cash flows from a bond, where the weights are the present values of each cash flow. The expression at (2.19) gives us the approximate measure of the change in price for a small change in yield. If we divide both sides of (2.19) by P we obtain the expression for the approximate percentage price change, given at (2.20).

$$\frac{dP}{dr}\frac{1}{P} = -\frac{1}{(1+r)} \left[\frac{1C}{(1+r)} + \frac{2C}{(1+r)^2} + \cdots\cdots + \frac{nC}{(1+r)^n} + \frac{nM}{(1+r)^n} \right] \frac{1}{P} \tag{2.20}$$

If we divide the bracketed expression in (2.20) by the current price of the bond P we obtain the definition of Macaulay duration, given at (2.21).

$$D = \frac{\frac{1C}{(1+r)} + \frac{2C}{(1+r)^2} + \cdots\cdots + \frac{nC}{(1+r)^n} + \frac{nM}{(1+r)^n}}{P} \tag{2.21}$$

Equation (2.21) is simplified using Σ notation as shown by (2.22).

$$D = \frac{\sum_{n=1}^{N} \frac{nC_n}{(1+r)^n}}{P} \tag{2.22}$$

where C represents the bond cash flow at time n.

Example 2.10 calculates the Macaulay duration for a hypothetical bond, an 8% 2009 annual coupon bond.

Example 2.10
Calculating the Macaulay duration for an 8% 2009 annual coupon bond

Issued	30 September 1999
Maturity	30 September 2009
Price	102.497
Yield	7.634%

Period (n)	Cash flow	PV at current yield[*]	$n \times$ PV
1	8	7.43260	7.4326
2	8	6.90543	13.81086
3	8	6.41566	19.24698
4	8	5.96063	23.84252
5	8	5.53787	27.68935
6	8	5.14509	30.87054
7	8	4.78017	33.46119
8	8	4.44114	35.529096
9	8	4.12615	37.13535
10	108	51.75222	517.5222
Total		102.49696	746.540686

[*]Calculated as $C/(1 + r)n$.
Macaulay Duration = 746.540686/102.497 = 7.283539998 years.
Modified Duration = 7.28354/1.07634 = 6.76695.

Table 2.4: Duration calculation for the 8% 2009 bond.

The Macaulay duration value given by (2.22) is measured in years. An interesting observation by Galen Burghardt in *The Treasury Bond Basis* is that, "measured in years, Macaulay's duration is of no particular use to anyone." (Burghardt 1994, page 90). This is essentially correct. However, as a risk measure and hedge calculation measure, duration transformed into *modified duration* was the primary measure of interest rate risk used in the markets, and is still widely used despite the advent of the *value-at-risk* measure for market risk.

If we substitute the expression for Macaulay duration (2.21) into equation (2.20) for the approximate percentage change in price we obtain (2.23) below.

$$\frac{dP}{dr}\frac{1}{P} = -\frac{1}{(1 + r)}D \tag{2.23}$$

This is the definition of modified duration, given as (2.24).

$$MD = \frac{D}{(1 + r)} \tag{2.24}$$

Modified duration is clearly related to duration then, in fact we can use it to indicate that, for small changes in yield, a given change in yield results in an inverse change in bond price. We can illustrate this by substituting (2.24) into (2.23), giving us (2.25).

$$\frac{dP}{dr}\frac{1}{P} = -MD \tag{2.25}$$

If we are determining duration long-hand, there is another arrangement we can use to shorten the procedure. Instead of equation (2.17) we use (2.26) as the bond price formula, which calculates price based on a bond being comprised of an annuity stream and a redemption payment, and summing the present values of these two elements. Again we assume an annual coupon bond priced on a date that leaves a complete number of years to maturity and with no interest accrued.

$$P = C\left[\frac{1 - \frac{1}{(1+r)^n}}{r}\right] + \frac{M}{(1+r)^n} \tag{2.26}$$

This expression calculates the price of a bond as the present value of the stream of coupon payments and the present value of the redemption payment. If we take the first derivative of (2.26) and then divide this by the current price of the bond P, the result is another expression for the modified duration formula, given at (2.27).

$$MD = \frac{\frac{C}{r^2}\left[1 - \frac{1}{(1+r)^n}\right] + \frac{n\left(M - \frac{C}{r}\right)}{(1+r)^{n+1}}}{P} \tag{2.27}$$

We have already shown that modified duration and duration are related; to obtain the expression for Macaulay duration from (2.27) we multiply it by $(1 + r)$. This short-hand formula is demonstrated in Example 2.11 for a hypothetical bond, the annual coupon 8% 2009.

Example 2.11

8% 2009 bond: using equation (2.27) for the modified duration calculation

Coupon	8%, annual basis
Yield	7.634%
N	10
Price	102.497

Substituting the above terms into the equation we obtain:

$$MD = \frac{\frac{8}{(0.07634^2)}\left[1 - \frac{1}{(1.07634)^{10}}\right] + \frac{10\left(100 - \frac{8}{0.07634}\right)}{(1.07634)}}{102.497}$$

$$= 6076695$$

To obtain the Macaulay duration we multiply the modified duration by $(1 + r)$, in this case 1.07634, which gives us a value of 7.28354 years.

For an irredeemable bond duration is given by:

$$D = \frac{1}{rc} \tag{2.28}$$

where $rc = (C/P_d)$ is the *running yield* (or *current yield*) of the bond. This follows from equation (2.22) as $N \to \infty$, recognising that for an irredeemable bond $r = rc$. Equation (2.28) provides the limiting value to duration. For bonds trading at or above par duration increases with maturity and approaches this limit from below. For bonds trading at a discount to par duration increases to a maximum at around 20 years and then declines towards the limit given by (2.28). So in general, duration increases with maturity, with an upper bound given by (2.28).

2.10.2 Properties of Macaulay duration

A bond's duration is always less than its maturity. This is because some weight is given to the cash flows in the early years of the bond's life, which brings forward the average time at which cash flows are received. In the case of a zero-coupon bond, there is no present value weighting of the cash flows, for the simple reason that there are no cash flows, and so duration for a zero-coupon bond is equal to its term to maturity. Duration varies with coupon, yield and maturity. The following three factors imply higher duration for a bond:

■ the lower the coupon;
■ the lower the yield;
■ broadly, the longer the maturity.

Duration increases as coupon and yield decrease. As the coupon falls, more of the relative weight of the cash flows is transferred to the maturity date and this causes duration to rise. Because the coupon on index-linked bonds is generally much lower than on vanilla bonds, this means that the duration of index-linked bonds will be much higher than for vanilla bonds of the same maturity. As yield increases, the present values of all future cash flows fall, but the present values of the more distant cash flows fall relatively more than those of the nearer cash flows. This has the effect of increasing the relative weight given to nearer cash flows and hence of reducing duration.

The effect of the coupon frequency

Certain bonds such as Eurobonds pay coupons annually compared to say, gilts which pay semi-annual coupons. If we imagine that every coupon is divided into two parts, with one part paid a half-period earlier than the other, this will represent a shift in weight to the left, as part of the coupon is paid earlier. Thus, increasing the coupon frequency shortens duration, and of course decreasing coupon frequency has the effect of lengthening duration.

Duration as maturity approaches

Using our definition of duration we can see that initially it will decline slowly, and then at a more rapid pace as a bond approaches maturity.

Duration of a portfolio

Portfolio duration is a weighted average of the duration of the individual bonds. The weights are the present values of the bonds divided by the full price of the entire portfolio, and the resulting duration calculation is often referred to as a "market-weighted" duration. This approach is in effect the duration calculation for a single bond. Portfolio duration has the same application as duration for an individual bond, and can be used to structure an *immunised* portfolio.

2.10.3 Modified duration

Although it is common for newcomers to the market to think intuitively of duration much as Macaulay originally did, as a proxy measure for the time to maturity of a bond, such an interpretation is to miss the main point of duration, which is a measure of price volatility or interest rate risk.

Using the first term of a Taylor's expansion of the bond price function[6] we can show the following relationship between price volatility and the duration measure, which is expressed as (2.29) below.

$$\Delta P = - \left[\frac{1}{(1+r)} \right] \times \text{Macaulay duration} \times \text{Change in yield} \qquad (2.29)$$

where r is the yield to maturity for an annual-paying bond (for a semi-annual coupon bond, we use $r/2$). If we combine the first two components of the right-hand side, we obtain the definition of modified duration. Equation (2.29) expresses the approximate percentage change in price as being equal to the modified duration multiplied by the change in yield. We saw in the previous section how the formula for Macaulay duration could be modified to obtain the *modified duration* for a bond. There is a clear relationship between the two measures. From the Macaulay duration of a bond can be derived its modified duration, which gives a measure of the sensitivity of a bond's price to small changes in yield. As we have seen, the relationship between modified duration and duration is given by (2.30).

$$MD = \frac{D}{1+r} \qquad (2.30)$$

where MD is the modified duration in years. However, it also measures the approximate change in bond price for a 1% change in bond yield. For a bond that pays semi-annual coupons, the equation becomes:

$$MD = \frac{D}{1 + \frac{1}{2}r} \qquad (2.31)$$

---

[6] For an accessible explanation of the Taylor expansion, see Butler, C., *Mastering Value-at-Risk*, FT Prentice Hall 1998, pp. 112–114.

This means that the following relationship holds between modified duration and bond prices:

$$\Delta P = MD \times \Delta r \times P \tag{2.32}$$

In the UK markets the term *volatility* is sometimes used to refer to modified duration but this is becoming increasingly uncommon in order to avoid confusion with option markets' use of the same term, which there often refers to *implied volatility* and is something different.

Example 2.12   Using modified duration

An 8% annual coupon bond is trading at par with a duration of 2.74 years. If yields rise from 8% to 8.50%, then the price of the bond will fall by:

$$\Delta P = -D \times \frac{\Delta r}{1+r} \times P$$
$$= -(2.74) \times \left(\frac{0.005}{1.080}\right) \times 100$$
$$= -1.2685$$

That is, the price of the bond will now be £98.7315.

The modified duration of a bond with a duration of 2.74 years and yield of 8% is obviously:

$$MD = \frac{2.74}{1.08}$$

which gives us *MD* equal to 2.537 years.

This tells us that for a 1 per cent move in the yield to maturity, the price of the bond will move (in the opposite direction) by 2.54%.

We can use modified duration to approximate bond prices for a given yield change. This is illustrated with the following expression:

$$\Delta P = -MD \times (\Delta r) \times P \tag{2.33}$$

For a bond with a modified duration of 3.99, priced at par, an increase in yield of 1 basis point (100 basis = 1 per cent) leads to a fall in the bond's price of:

$$\Delta P = (-3.24/100) \times (+0.01) \times 100.00$$
$$\Delta P = 0.0399, \text{ or } 3.99 \text{ pence}$$

In this case 3.99 pence is the *basis point value* of the bond, which is the change in the bond price given a 1 basis point change in the bond's yield. The basis point value of a bond can be calculated using (2.34).

$$BPV = \frac{MD}{100} \times \frac{P}{100} \qquad (2.34)$$

Basis point values are used in hedging bond positions. To hedge a bond position requires an opposite position to be taken in the hedging instrument. So if we are long a 10-year bond, we may wish to sell short a similar 10-year bond as a hedge against it. Similarly a short position in a bond will be hedged through a purchase of an equivalent amount of the hedging instrument. In fact there are a variety of hedging instruments available, both on and off-balance sheet. Once the hedge is put on, any loss in the primary position should in theory be offset by a gain in the hedge position, and vice-versa. The objective of a hedge is to ensure that the price change in the primary instrument is equal to the price change in the hedging instrument. If we are hedging a position with another bond, we use the BPVs of each bond to calculate the amount of the hedging instrument required. This is important because each bond will have different BPVs, so that to hedge a long position in say £1 million nominal of a 30-year bond does not mean we simply sell £1 million of another 30-year bond. This is because the BPVs of the two bonds will almost certainly be different. Also there may not be another 30-year bond in that particular bond. What if we have to hedge with a 10-year bond? How much nominal of this bond would be required?

We need to know the ratio given at (2.35) to calculate the nominal hedge position.

$$\frac{BPV_p}{BPV_h} \qquad (2.35)$$

where

BPV_p is the basis point value of the primary bond (the position to be hedged)

BPV_h is the basis point value of the hedging instrument.

The *hedge ratio* is used to calculate the size of the hedge position and is given at (2.36).

$$\frac{BPV_p}{BPV_h} \times \frac{\text{change in yield for primary bond position}}{\text{change in yield for hedge instrument}} \qquad (2.36)$$

The second ratio in (2.36) is known as the *yield beta*.

Example 2.13 illustrates using the hedge ratio.

Example 2.13   Calculating hedge size using basis point value

A trader holds a long position of £1 million of the 8% 2019 bond. The modified duration of the bond is 11.14692 and its price is 129.87596. The basis point value of this bond is therefore 0.14477. The trader decides, to protect against a rise in interest rates, to hedge the position using the 0% 2009 bond, which has a BPV of 0.05549. If we assume that the yield beta is 1, what nominal value of the zero-coupon bond must be sold in order to hedge the position?

The hedge ratio is:

$$\frac{0.14477}{0.05549} \times 1 = 2.60894.$$

Therefore to hedge £1 million of the 20-year bond the trader shorts £2,608,940 of the zero-coupon bond. If we use the respective BPVs to see the net effect of a 1 basis point rise in yield, the loss on the long position is approximately equal to the gain in the hedge position.

Example 2.14   The nature of the modified duration approximation

Table 2.5 shows the change in price for one of our hypothetical bonds, the 8% 2009, for a selection of yields. We see that for a 1 basis point change in yield, the change in price given by the dollar duration figure, while not completely accurate, is a reasonable estimation of the actual change in price. For a large move however, say 200 basis points, the approximation is significantly in error and analysts would not use it. Notice also for our hypothetical bond how the dollar duration value, which is the suggested change in cash value resulting from the change in yields calculated from the modified duration measurement, underestimates the change in price resulting from a fall in yields but overestimates the price change for a rise in yields. This is a reflection of the price/yield relationship for this bond. Some bonds will have a more pronounced convex relationship between price and yield and the modified duration calculation will underestimate the price change resulting from both a fall or a rise in yields.

2.10.4 Convexity

Duration can be regarded as a first-order measure of interest rate risk: it measures the *slope* of the present value/yield profile. It is, however, only an approximation of the actual change in bond price given a small change in yield to maturity. Similarly for modified duration, which describes the price sensitivity of a bond to small changes in yield. However, as Figure 2.3 illustrates, the approximation is an underestimate of the actual price at the new yield. This is the weakness of the duration measure.

Bond	Maturity (years)	Modified Duration	Price duration of basis point	Yield									
				6.00%	6.50%	7.00%	7.50%	7.99%	8.00%	8.01%	8.50%	9.00%	10.00%
8%2009	10	6.76695	0.06936	114.72017	110.78325	107.02358	103.43204	100.06713	100.00000	99.932929	96.71933	93.58234	87.71087

Yield change	Price change	Estimate using price duration
down 1 bp	0.06713	0.06936
up 1 pb	0.06707	0.06936
down 200 bp	14.72017	13.872
up 200 pb	12.28913	13.872

Table 2.5: Nature of the modified duration approximation.

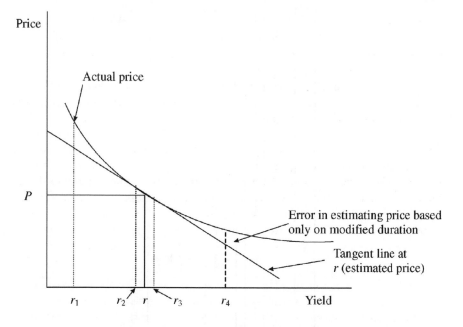

Figure 2.3: Approximation of the bond price change using modified
duration. Reproduced with permission from Frank J Fabozzi, *Fixed
Income Mathematics*, McGraw-Hill 1997.

Convexity is a second-order measure of interest rate risk; it measures the
curvature of the present value/yield profile. Convexity can be regarded as an
indication of the error we make when using duration and modified duration, as it
measures the degree to which the curvature of a bond's price/yield relationship
diverges from the straight-line estimation. The convexity of a bond is positively
related to the dispersion of its cash flows thus, other things being equal, if one
bond's cash flows are more spread out in time than another's, then it will have a
higher *dispersion* and hence a higher convexity. Convexity is also positively related
to duration.

The second-order differential of the bond price equation with respect to the
redemption yield r is:

$$\frac{\Delta P}{P} = \frac{1}{P}\frac{\Delta P}{\Delta r}(\Delta r) + \frac{1}{2P}\frac{\Delta^2 P}{\Delta r^2}(\Delta r^2)$$
$$= -MD\left(\Delta r + \frac{CV}{2}\right)(\Delta r)^2 \qquad (2.37)$$

where *CV* is the convexity.

From equation (2.37), convexity is the rate at which price variation to yield changes with respect to yield. That is, it describes a bond's modified duration changes with respect to changes in yield. It can be approximated by expression (2.38).

$$CV = 10^8 \left(\frac{\Delta P'}{P} + \frac{\Delta P''}{P} \right) \tag{2.38}$$

where

$\Delta P'$ is the change in bond price if yield increases by 1 basis point (0.01)

$\Delta P''$ is the change in bond price if yield decreases by 1 basis point (0.01).

The unit of measurement for convexity using (2.38) is the number of interest periods. For annual coupon bonds this is equal to the number of years; for bonds paying coupon on a different frequency we use (2.39) to convert the convexity measure to years.

$$CV_{years} = \frac{CV}{C^2} \tag{2.39}$$

The convexity measure for a zero-coupon bond is given by (2.40).

$$CV = \frac{n(n+1)}{(1+r)^2} \tag{2.40}$$

Convexity is a second-order approximation of the change in price resulting from a change in yield. This is given by:

$$\Delta P = \frac{1}{2} \times CV \times (\Delta r)^2 \tag{2.41}$$

The reason we multiply the convexity by 1/2 to obtain the convexity adjustment is because the second term in the Taylor expansion contains the coefficient 1/2. The convexity approximation is obtained from a Taylor expansion of the bond price formula. An illustration of Taylor expansion of the bond price/yield equation is given in Appendix 39.3 of the author's book *The Bond and Money Markets*. The formula is the same for a semi-annual coupon bond.

Note that the value for convexity given by the expressions above will always be positive, that is the approximate price change due to convexity is positive for both yield increases and decreases.

Convexity is an attractive property for a bond to have. What level of premium will be attached to a bond's higher convexity? This is a function of the current yield levels in the market as well as market volatility. Remember that modified duration and convexity are functions of yield level, and that the effect of both is magnified at lower yield levels. As well as the relative level, investors will value convexity higher if the current market conditions are volatile. Remember that the cash effect of convexity is noticeable only for large moves in yield. If an investor expects market yields to move only by relatively small amounts, they will attach a lower value to convexity; and vice-versa for large movements in yield. Therefore the yield premium attached to a bond with higher convexity will vary according to market expectations of the future size of interest rate changes.

The convexity measure increases with the square of maturity, and it decreases with both coupon and yield. As the measure is a function of modified duration, index-linked bonds have greater convexity than conventional bonds. We discussed how the price/yield profile will be more convex for a bond of higher convexity, and that such a bond will outperform a bond of lower convexity whatever happens to market interest rates. High convexity is therefore a desirable property for bonds to have. In principle a more convex bond should fall in price less than a less convex one when yields rise, and rise in price more when yields fall. That is, convexity can be equated with the potential to outperform. Thus, other things being equal, the higher the convexity of a bond the more desirable it should, in principle, be to investors. In some cases investors may be prepared to accept a bond with a lower yield in order to gain convexity. We noted also that convexity is in principle of more value if uncertainty, and hence expected market volatility, is high, because the convexity effect of a bond is amplified for large changes in yield. The value of convexity is therefore greater in volatile market conditions.

For a conventional vanilla bond convexity is almost always positive. Negative convexity resulting from a bond with a concave price/yield profile would not be an attractive property for a bondholder; the most common occurrence of negative convexity in the cash markets is with callable bonds.

Selected references and bibliography

Baxter, M., Rennie, A., *Financial Calculus*, Cambridge University Press 1996

Bierwag, G.O., "Immunization, duration and the term structure of interest rates," *Journal of Financial and Quantitative Analysis*, December 1977, pp. 725–741

Bierwag, G.O., "Measures of duration," *Economic Inquiry 16*, October 1978, pp. 497–507

Burghardt, G., *The Treasury Bond Basis*, McGraw-Hill 1994

Choudhry, M., *The Bond and Money Markets: Strategy, Trading, Analysis*, Butterworth-Heinemann 2001, Chapters 2–10, 39

Fabozzi, F., *Bond Markets, Analysis and Strategies*, Prentice Hall 1989, Chapter 2

Garbade, K., *Fixed Income Analytics*, MIT Press 1996, Chapters 3, 4 and 12

Hull, J., *Options, Futures and Other Derivatives*, 3rd edition, Prentice Hall 1997

Jarrow, R., *Modelling Fixed Income Securities and Interest Rate Options*, McGraw-Hill 1996

Macaulay, F., *The Movements of Interest Rates, Bond Yields and Stock Prices in the United States Since 1856*, RISK Classics Library 1999

Neftci, S., *Mathematics of Financial Derivatives*, Academic Press 1996

Steiner, R., *Mastering Financial Calculations*, FT Pitman 1998

3 Bond Futures

A widely used risk management instrument in the bond markets is the government bond futures contract. This is an exchange-traded standardised contract that fixes the price today at which a specified quantity and quality of a bond will be delivered at a date during the expiry month of the futures contract. Unlike short-term interest rate futures, which only require cash settlement, bond futures require the actual physical delivery of a bond when they are settled.

In this chapter we review bond futures contracts and their use for trading and hedging purposes.

3.1 Introduction

A *futures contract* is an agreement between two counterparties that fixes the terms of an exchange that will take place between them at some future date. They are standardised agreements as opposed to "over-the-counter" or OTC ones, as they are traded on an exchange, so they are also referred to as *exchange traded futures*. In the UK financial futures are traded on LIFFE, the London International Financial Futures Exchange which opened in 1982. LIFFE is the biggest financial futures exchange in Europe in terms of volume of contracts traded. There are four classes of contract traded on LIFFE: short-term interest rate contracts, long-term interest rate contracts (bond futures), currency contracts and stock index contracts.

Bond futures contracts, which are an important part of the bond markets, they are used for hedging and speculative purposes. Most futures contracts on exchanges around the world trade at three-month maturity intervals, with maturity dates fixed at March, June, September and December each year. This includes the contracts traded on LIFFE. Therefore at pre-set times during the year a contract for each of these months will *expire*, and a final *settlement* price is determined for it. The further out one goes the less liquid the trading is in that contract. It is normal to see liquid trading only in the *front month* contract (the current contract, so that if we are trading in April 2002 the front month is the June 2002 future), and possibly one or two of the next contracts, for most bond futures contracts. The liquidity of contracts diminishes the further one trades out in the maturity range.

When a party establishes a position in a futures contract, it can either run this position to maturity or close out the position between trade date and maturity. If a position is closed out the party will have either a profit or loss to book. If a position is held until maturity, the party who is long futures will take delivery of the underlying asset (bond) at the settlement price; the party who is short futures will deliver the underlying asset. This is referred to as *physical settlement* or sometimes, confusingly, as *cash settlement*.

There is no counterparty risk associated with trading exchange-traded futures, because of the role of the *clearing house*, such as the London Clearing House. This is the body through which contracts are settled. A clearing house acts as the buyer to all contracts sold on the exchange, and the seller to all contracts that are bought. So in the London market the LCH acts as the counterparty to all transactions, so that settlement is effectively guaranteed. The LCH requires all exchange participants to deposit *margin* with it, a cash sum that is the cost of conducting business (plus brokers' commissions). The size of the margin depends on the size of a party's net *open* position in contracts (an open position is a position in a contract that is held overnight and not closed out). There are two types of margin, *maintenance margin* and *variation margin*. Maintenance margin is the minimum level required to be held at the clearing house; the level is set by the exchange. Variation margin is the additional amount that must be deposited to cover any trading losses and as the size of the net open positions increases. Note that this is not like margin in say, a repo transaction. Margin in repo is a safeguard against a drop in value of collateral that has been supplied against a loan of cash. The margin deposited at a futures exchange clearing house acts essentially as "good faith" funds, required to provide comfort to the exchange that the futures trader is able to satisfy the obligations of the futures contract.

3.1.1 Contract specifications

We have noted that futures contracts traded on an exchange are standardised. This means that each contract represents exactly the same commodity, and it cannot be tailored to meet individual customer requirements. In this section we describe two very liquid and commonly traded contracts, starting with the US T-bond contract traded on the Chicago Board of Trade (CBOT). The details of this contract are given in Table 3.1.

The terms of this contract relate to a US Treasury bond with a minimum maturity of 15 years and a *notional* coupon of 8%. We introduced the concept of the notional bond in the chapter on repo markets. A futures contract specifies a notional coupon to prevent delivery and liquidity problems that would arise if there was shortage of bonds with exactly the coupon required, or if one market participant purchased a large proportion of all the bonds in issue with the required coupon. For exchange-traded futures, a short future can deliver any bond that fits the maturity criteria specified in the contract terms. Of course a long future would like to deliver a high-coupon bond with significant accrued interest, while the short future would want to deliver a low-coupon bond with low interest accrued.

Unit of trading	US Treasury bond with notional value of $100,000 and a coupon of 8%
Deliverable grades	US T-bonds with a minimum maturity of 15 years from first day of delivery month
Delivery months	March, June, September, December
Delivery date	Any business day during the delivery month
Last trading day	12:00 noon, seventh business day before last business day of delivery month
Quotation	Per cent of par expressed as points and thirty-seconds of a point, e.g., 108–16 is 108 16/32 or 108.50
Minimum price movement	1/32
Tick value	$31.25
Trading hours	07:20–14:00 (trading pit)
	17:20–20:05
	22:30–06:00 hours (screen trading)

Source: CBOT

Table 3.1: CBOT US T-bond futures contract.

In fact this issue does not arise because of the way the *invoice amount* (the amount paid by the long future to purchase the bond) is calculated. The invoice amount on the expiry date is given as equation (3.1):

$$Inv_{amt} = P_{fut} \times CF + AI$$

where

Inv_{amt}	is the invoice amount;
P_{fut}	is the price of the futures contract;
CF	is the conversion factor;
AI	is the bond accrued interest.

Any bond that meets the maturity specifications of the futures contract is said to be in the *delivery basket*, the group of bonds that are eligible to be delivered into the futures contract. Every bond in the delivery basket will have its own *conversion factor*, which is used to equalise coupon and accrued interest differences of all the delivery bonds. The exchange will announce the conversion factor for each bond before trading in a contract begins; the conversion factor for a bond will change over time, but remains fixed for one individual contract. That is, if a bond has a conversion factor of 1.091252, this will remain fixed for the life of the contract. If a contract specifies a bond with a notional coupon of 7%, like the long gilt future on LIFFE, then the conversion factor will be less than 1.0 for bonds with a coupon lower than 7% and higher than 1.0 for bonds with a coupon higher than 7%. A formal definition of conversion factor is given below.

Conversion factor

The conversion factor (or price factor) gives the price of an individual cash bond such that its yield to maturity on the delivery day of the futures contract is equal to the notional coupon of the contract. The product of the conversion factor and the futures price is the forward price available in the futures market for that cash bond (plus the cost of funding, referred to as the gross basis).

Although conversion factors equalise the yield on bonds, bonds in the delivery basket will trade at different yields, and for this reason they are not "equal" at the time of delivery. Certain bonds will be cheaper than others, and one bond will be the *cheapest-to-deliver* bond. The cheapest-to-deliver bond is the one that gives the greatest return from a strategy of buying a bond and simultaneously selling the futures contract, and then closing out positions on the expiry of the contract. This so-called *cash-and-carry trading* is actively pursued by proprietary trading desks in banks. If a contract is purchased and then held to maturity the buyer will receive, via the exchange's clearing house the cheapest-to-deliver gilt. Traders sometimes try to exploit arbitrage price differentials between the future and the cheapest-to-deliver gilt, known as *basis trading*.

The mathematical calculation of the conversion factor for the gilt future is given in Appendix 3.1.

We summarise the contract specification of the long gilt futures contract traded on LIFFE in Table 3.2. There is also a medium gilt contract on LIFFE, which was

Unit of trading	UK gilt bond having a face value of £100,000, a notional coupon of 7% and a notional maturity of 10 years (changed from contract value of £50,000 from the September 1998 contract)
Deliverable grades	UK gilts with a maturity ranging from $8\frac{3}{4}$ to 13 years from the first day of the delivery month (changed from 10–15 years from the December 1998 contract)
Delivery months	March, June, September, December
Delivery date	Any business day during the delivery month
Last trading day	11:00 hours, two business days before last business day of delivery month
Quotation	Per cent of par expressed as points and hundredths of a point, for example 114.56 (changed from ticks and 1/32nds of a point, as in 117–17 meaning 114 17/32 or 114.53125, from the June 1998 contract)
Minimum price movement	0.01 of one point (one tick)
Tick value	£10
Trading hours	08:00–18:00 hours All trading conducted electronically on LIFFE CONNECT™ platform

Source: LIFFE

Table 3.2: LIFFE long gilt future contract specification.

introduced in 1998 (having been discontinued in the early 1990s). This trades a notional five-year gilt, with eligible gilts being those of four to seven years' maturity.

3.2   Futures pricing

3.2.1 Theoretical principle

Although it may not appear so on first trading, floor trading on a futures exchange is probably the closest one gets to an example of the economist's perfect and efficient market. The immediacy and liquidity of the market will ensure that at virtually all times the price of any futures contract reflects fair value. In essence because a futures contract represents an underlying asset, albeit a synthetic one, its price cannot differ from the actual cash market price of the asset itself. This is because the market sets futures prices such that they are arbitrage-free. We can illustrate this with a hypothetical example.

Let us say that the benchmark 10-year bond, with a coupon of 8% is trading at par. This bond is the underlying asset represented by the long bond futures contract; the front month contract expires in precisely three months. If we also say that the three-month LIBOR rate (the repo rate) is 6%, what is fair value for the front month futures contract?

For the purpose of illustration let us start by assuming the futures price to be 105. We could carry out the following arbitrage-type trade:

■ buy the bond for £100;
■ simultaneously sell the future at £105;
■ borrow £100 for three months at the repo rate of 6%.

As this is a leveraged trade we have borrowed the funds with which to buy the bond, and the loan is fixed at three months because we will hold the position to the futures contract expiry, which is in exactly three months' time. At expiry, as we are short futures we will deliver the underlying bond to the futures clearing house and close out the loan. This strategy will result in cash flows for us as shown below.

> *Futures settlement cash flows*
> Price received for bond   =   105.00
> Bond accrued   =   2.00 (8% coupon for three months)
> Total proceeds   =   107.00
> *Loan cash flows*
> Repayment of principal   =   100.00
> Loan interest   =   1.500 (6% repo rate for three months)
> Total outlay   =   101.50

The trade has resulted in a profit of £5.50, and this profit is guaranteed as we have traded the two positions simultaneously and held them both to maturity. We are not affected by subsequent market movements. The trade is an example of a pure arbitrage, which is risk-free. There is no cash outflow at the start of the trade because we borrowed the funds used to buy the bond. In essence we have locked in the forward price of the bond by trading the future today, so that the final settlement price of the futures contract is irrelevant. If the situation described above were to occur in practice it would be very short-lived, precisely because arbitrageurs would buy the bond and sell the future to make this profit. This activity would force changes in the prices of both bond and future until the profit opportunity was removed.

So in our illustration the price of the future was too high (and possibly the price of the bond was too low as well) and not reflecting fair value because the price of the synthetic asset was out of line with the cash asset.

What if the price of the future was too low? Let us imagine that the futures contract is trading at 95.00. We could then carry out the following trade:

- sell the bond at £100;
- simultaneously buy the future for £95;
- lend the proceeds of the short sale (£100) for three months at 6%.

This trade has the same procedure as the first one with no initial cash outflow, except that we have to cover the short position in the repo market, through which we invest the sale proceeds at the repo rate of 6%. After three months we are delivered a bond as part of the futures settlement, and this is used to close out our short position. How has our strategy performed?

Futures settlement cash flows
Clean price of bond	=	95.00
Bond accrued	=	2.00
Total cash outflow	=	97.00

Loan cash flows
Principal on loan maturity	=	100.00
Interest from loan	=	1.500
Total cash inflow	=	101.500

The profit of £4.50 is again a risk-free arbitrage profit. Of course our hypothetical world has ignored considerations such as bid–offer spreads for the bond, future and repo rates, which would apply in the real world and impact on any trading strategy. Yet again however the futures price is out of line with the cash market and has provided opportunity for arbitrage profit.

Given the terms and conditions that apply in our example, there is one price for the futures contract at which no arbitrage profit opportunity is available. If we set the future price at 99.5, we would see that both trading strategies, buying the bond and selling the future or selling the bond and buying the future, yield a net cash flow of zero. There is no profit to be made from either strategy. So at 99.5 the futures price is in line with the cash market, and it will only move as the cash market price moves; any other price will result in an arbitrage profit opportunity.

3.2.2 Arbitrage-free futures pricing

The previous section demonstrated how we can arrive at the fair value for a bond futures contract provided we have certain market information. The market mechanism and continuous trading will ensure that the fair price *is* achieved, as arbitrage profit opportunities are eliminated. We can determine the bond future's price given:

- the coupon of the underlying bond, and its price in the cash market;
- the interest rate for borrowing or lending funds, from the trade date to the maturity date of the futures contract. This is known as the *repo* rate.

For the purpose of deriving this pricing model we can ignore bid–offer spreads and borrowing and lending spreads. We set the following:

r	is the repo rate;
rc	is the bond's running yield;
P_{bond}	is the price of the cash bond;
P_{fut}	is the price of the futures contract;
t	is the time to the expiry of the futures contract.

We can substitute these symbols into the cash flow profile for our earlier trade strategy, that of buying the bond and selling the future. This gives us:

Futures settlement cash flows

Clean price for bond	$=$	P_{fut}
Bond accrued	$-$	$rc \times t \times P_{bond}$
Total proceeds	$=$	$P_{fut} + (rc \times t \times P_{bond})$

loan cash flows

repayment of loan principal	$=$	P_{bond}
Loan interest	$=$	$r \times t \times P_{bond}$
Total outlay	$=$	$P_{bond} + (r \times t \times P_{bond})$

The profit from the trade would be the difference between the proceeds and outlay, which we can set as follows:

$$\text{Profit} = P_{fut} + rc \times t \times P_{bond} - P_{bond} + r \times t \times P_{bond} \qquad (3.2)$$

We have seen how the futures price is at fair value when there is no profit to be gained from carrying out this trade, so if we set profit at zero, we obtain the following:

$$0 = P_{fut} + rc \times t \times P_{bond} - P_{bond} + r \times t \times P_{bond}$$

Solving this expression for the futures price P_{fut} gives us.

$$P_{fut} = P_{bond} + P_{bond}\,t(r - rc).$$

Rearranging this we get:

$$P_{fut} = P_{bond}(1 + t(r - rc)). \tag{3.3}$$

If we repeat the procedure for the other strategy, that of selling the bond and simultaneously buying the future, and set the profit to zero, we will obtain the same equation for the futures price as given in equation (3.3).

It is the level of the repo rate in the market, compared to the running yield on the underlying bond, that sets the price for the futures contract. From the examples used at the start of this section we can see that it is the cost of funding compared to the repo rate that determines if the trade strategy results in a profit. The equation $(r - rc)$ from (3.3) is the net financing cost in the arbitrage trade, and is known as the *cost of carry*. If the running yield on the bond is higher than the funding cost (the repo rate) this is positive funding or *positive carry*. Negative funding (*negative carry*) is when the repo rate is higher than the running yield. The level of $(r - rc)$ will determine whether the futures price is trading above the cash market price or below it. If we have positive carry (when $rc < r$) then the futures price will trade below the cash market price, known as trading at a *discount*. Where $r > rc$ and we have negative carry then the futures price will be at a premium over the cash market price. If the net funding cost was zero, such that we had neither positive nor negative carry, then the futures price would be equal to the underlying bond price.

The cost of carry related to a bond futures contract is a function of the yield curve. In a positive yield curve environment the three-month repo rate is likely to be lower than the running yield on a bond so that the cost of carry is likely to be positive. As there is generally only a liquid market in long bond futures out to contracts that mature up to one year from the trade date, with a positive yield curve it would be unusual to have a short-term repo rate higher than the running yield on the long bond. So in such an environment we would have the future trading at a discount to the underlying cash bond. If there is a negative sloping yield curve the futures price will trade at a premium to the cash price. It is in circumstances of changes in the shape of the yield curve that opportunities for relative value and arbitrage trading arise, especially as the bond that is cheapest-to-deliver for the futures contract may change with large changes in the curve.

A trading strategy that involved simultaneous and opposite positions in the cheapest-to-deliver bond (CTD) and the futures contract is known as *cash-and-carry* trading or *basis trading*. However, by the law of no-arbitrage pricing, the payoff from such a trading strategy should be zero. If we set the profit from such a trading strategy as zero, we can obtain a pricing formula for the fair value of a futures contract, which summarises the discussion above, and states that the fair value futures price is a function of the cost of carry on the underlying bond. This is given as equation (3.4):

$$P_{fut} = \frac{(P_{bond} + AI_0) \times (1 + rt) - \sum_{i=1}^{N} C_i(1 + rt_{i,del}) - AI_{del}}{CF} \qquad (3.4)$$

where

AI_0 is the accrued interest on the underlying bond today;

AI_{del} is the accrued interest on the underlying bond on the expiry or delivery date (assuming the bond is delivered on the final day, which will be the case if the running yield on the bond is above the money market rate);

C_i is the ith coupon;

N is the number of coupons paid from today to the expiry or delivery date;

r is the repo rate;

t is the time period (in years) over which the trade takes place;

CF is the bond conversion factor;

$ti_{,del}$ is the period from receipt of the ith coupon to delivery.

3.3   Hedging using bond futures

3.3.1 Introduction

Bond futures are used for a variety of purposes. Much of one day's trading in futures will be speculative, that is, a punt on the direction of the market. Another main use of futures is to hedge bond positions. In theory, if hedging a cash bond position with a bond futures contract, if cash and futures prices move together, then any loss from one position will be offset by a gain from the other. When prices move exactly in lock-step with each other, the hedge is considered perfect. In practice the price of even the cheapest-to-deliver bond (which one can view as being the bond being traded – implicitly – when one is trading the bond future) and the bond future will not move exactly in line with each other over a period of time. The difference between the cash price and the futures price is called the *basis*. The risk that the basis will change in an unpredictable way is known as *basis risk*.

Futures are a liquid and straightforward way of hedging a bond position. By hedging a bond position the trader or fund manager is hoping to balance the loss on the cash position by the profit gained from the hedge. However the hedge will not be exact for all bonds except the cheapest-to-deliver (CTD) bond, which we can assume is the futures contract underlying bond. The basis risk in a hedge position arises because the bond being hedged is not identical to the CTD bond.

The basic principle is that if the trader is long (or net long, where the desk is running long and short positions in different bonds) in the cash market, an equivalent number of futures contracts will be sold to set up the hedge. If the cash position is short the trader will buy futures. The hedging requirement can arise for different reasons. A market maker will wish to hedge positions arising out of client business, when they are unsure when the resulting bond positions will be unwound. A fund manager may, for example, know that they need to realise a cash sum at a specific time in the future to meet fund liabilities, and sell bonds at that time. The market maker will want to hedge against a drop in value of positions during the time the bonds are held. The fund manager will want to hedge against a rise in interest rates between now and the bond sale date, to protect the value of the portfolio.

When putting on the hedge position the key is to trade the correct number of futures contracts. This is determined by using the *hedge ratio* of the bond and the future, which is a function of the volatilities of the two instruments. The amount of contracts to trade is calculated using the hedge ratio, which is given by:

$$Hedge\ ratio = \frac{Volatility\ of\ bond\ to\ be\ hedged}{Volatility\ of\ hedging\ instrument}$$

Therefore one needs to use the volatility values of each instrument. We can see from the calculation that if the bond is more volatile than the hedging instrument, then a greater amount of the hedging instrument will be required. Let us now look in greater detail at the hedge ratio.

There are different methods available to calculate hedge ratios. The most common ones are the conversion factor method, which can be used for deliverable bonds (also known as the *price factor* method) and the modified duration method (also known as the basis point value method).

Where a hedge is put on against a bond that is in the futures delivery basket it is common for the conversion factor to be used to calculate the hedge ratio. A conversion factor hedge ratio is more useful as it is transparent and remains constant, irrespective of any changes in the price of the cash bond or the futures contract. The number of futures contracts required to hedge a deliverable bond using the conversion factor hedge ratio is determined using equation (3.5):

$$Number\ of\ contracts = \frac{M_{bond} \times CF}{M_{fut}} \tag{3.5}$$

where M is the nominal value of the bond or futures contract.

The conversion factor method may only be used for bonds in the delivery basket. It is important to ensure that this method is only used for one bond. It is an erroneous procedure to use the ratio of conversion factors of two different bonds when calculating a hedge ratio, as detailed in Galitz (1995) and elsewhere.

Unlike the conversion factor method, the modified duration hedge ratio may be used for all bonds, both deliverable and non-deliverable. In calculating this hedge ratio the modified duration is multiplied by the dirty price of the cash bond to obtain the *basis point value* (BPV). The BPV represents the actual impact of a change in the yield on the price of a specific bond. The BPV allows the trader to calculate the hedge ratio to reflect the different price sensitivity of the chosen bond (compared to the CTD bond) to interest rate movements. The hedge ratio calculated using BPVs must be constantly updated, because it will change if the price of the bond and/or the futures contract changes. This may necessitate periodic adjustments to the number of lots used in the hedge.

The number of futures contracts required to hedge a bond using the BPV method is calculated using the following:

$$Number\ of\ contracts = \frac{M_{bond}}{M_{fut}} \times \frac{BPV_{bond}}{BPV_{fut}} \quad (3.6)$$

where the BPV of a futures contract is defined with respect to the BPV of its CTD bond, as given by equation (3.7):

$$BPV_{fut} = \frac{BPV_{CTDbond}}{CF_{CTDbond}} \quad (3.7)$$

The simplest hedge procedure to undertake is one for a position consisting of only one bond, the cheapest-to-deliver bond. The relationship between the futures price and the price of the CTD given by equation (3.4) indicates that the price of the future will move for moves in the price of the CTD bond, so therefore we may set:

$$VP_{fut} \frac{VP_{Bond}}{CF} \quad (3.8)$$

where *CF* is the CTD conversion factor.

The price of the futures contract, over time, does not move tick-for-tick with the CTD bond (although it may on an intra-day basis) but rather by the amount of the change divided by the conversion factor. It is apparent therefore that to hedge a position in the CTD bond we must hold the number of futures contracts equivalent to the value of bonds held multiplied by the conversion factor. Obviously if a conversion factor is less than one, the number of futures contracts will be less than the equivalent nominal value of the cash position; the opposite is true for bonds that have a conversion factor greater than one. However the hedge is not as simple as dividing the nominal value of the bond position by the nominal value represented by one futures contract.

To measure the effectiveness of the hedge position, it is necessary to compare the performance of the futures position with that of the cash bond position, and to see how much the hedge instrument mirrored the performance of the cash instrument. A simple calculation is made to measure the effectiveness of the hedge, given by equation (3.9), which is the percentage value of the hedge effectiveness:

$$\text{Hedge effectiveness} = -\left(\frac{Fut\ p/l}{Bond\ p/l}\right) \times 100 \qquad (3.9)$$

3.3.2 Hedging a bond portfolio

The principles established above may be applied when hedging a portfolio containing a number of bonds. It is more realistic to consider a portfolio holding not just bonds that are outside the delivery basket, but are also not government bonds. In this case we need to calculate the number of futures contracts to put on as a hedge based on the volatility of each bond in the portfolio compared to the volatility of the CTD bond. Note that in practice, there is usually more than one futures contract that may be used as the hedge instrument. For example in the sterling market it would be more sensible to use LIFFE's medium gilt contract, whose underlying bond has a notional maturity of four to seven years, if hedging a portfolio of short- to medium-dated bonds. However for the purposes of illustration we will assume that only one contract, the long bond, is available.

To calculate the number of futures contracts required to hold as a hedge against any specific bond, we use equation (3.10).

$$Hedge = \frac{M_{bond}}{M_{fut}} \times Vol_{bond/CTD} \times Vol_{CTD/fut} \qquad (3.10)$$

where

M	is the nominal value of the bond or future;
$Vol_{bond/CTD}$	is the relative volatility of the bond being hedged compared to that of the CTD bond;
$Vol_{CTD/fut}$	is the relative volatility of the CTD bond compared to that of the future.

It is not necessarily straightforward to determine the relative volatility of a bond vis-à-vis the CTD bond. If the bond being hedged is a government bond, we can calculate the relative volatility using the two bonds' modified duration. This is because the yields of both may be safely assumed to be strongly positively correlated. If however the bond being hedged is a corporate bond and/or non-vanilla bond, we must obtain the relative volatility using regression analysis, as the yields between the two bonds may not be strongly positively correlated. This is apparent when one remembers that the yield spread of corporate bonds over government bonds is not constant, and will fluctuate with changes in government bond yields. To use regression analysis to determine relative volatilities, historical price data on the bond is required; the daily price moves in the target bond and the CTD bond are then analysed to assess the slope of the regression line. In this section we will restrict the discussion to a portfolio of government bonds.

If we are hedging a portfolio of government bonds we can use equation (3.11) to determine relative volatility values, based on the modified duration of each of the bonds in the portfolio.

$$\text{Vol}_{\text{bond/CTD}} = \frac{P_{bond}}{P_{CTD}} \approx \frac{MD_{bond} \times P_{bond}}{MD_{CTD} \times P_{CTD}} \tag{3.11}$$

where MD is the modified duration of the bond being hedged or the CTD bond, as appropriate.[1] Once we have calculated the relative volatility of the bond being hedged, equation (3.12) (obtained from (3.8) and (3.11)) tells us that the relative volatility of the CTD bond to that of the futures contract is approximately the same as its conversion factor. We are then in a position to calculate the futures hedge for each bond in a portfolio.

$$\text{Vol}_{\text{CTD/fut}} = \frac{P_{CTD}}{P_{fut}} \approx CF_{CTD} \tag{3.12}$$

Table 3.3 shows a portfolio of five UK gilts on 20 October 1999. The nominal value of the bonds in the portfolio is £200 million, and the bonds have a market value excluding accrued interest of £206.84 million. Only one of the bonds is a deliverable bond, the 5 $\frac{3}{4}$% 2009 gilt which is in fact the CTD bond. For the Dec '99 futures contract the bond had a conversion factor of 0.9124950. The fact that this bond is the CTD explains why it has a relative volatility of 1. We calculate the number of futures contracts required to hedge each position, using the equations listed above. For example, the hedge requirement for the position in the 7% 2002 gilt was calculated as follows:

$$\frac{5,000,000}{100,000} \times \frac{2.245 \times 101.50}{7.235 \times 99.84} \times 0.9124950 = 14.39$$

The volatility of all the bonds is calculated relative to the CTD bond, and the number of futures contracts determined using the conversion factor for the CTD

---

[1]   In certain textbooks and practitioner research documents, it is suggested that the ratio of the conversion factors of the bond being hedged (if it is in the delivery basket) and the CTD bond can be used to determine the relative volatility of the target bond. This is a specious argument. The conversion factor of a deliverable bond is the price factor that will set the yield of the bond equal to the notional coupon of the futures contract on the delivery date, and it is a function mainly of the coupon of the deliverable bond. The price volatility of a bond on the other hand, is a measure of its modified duration, which is a function of the bond's duration (that is, the weighted average term to maturity). Therefore using conversion factors to measure volatility levels will produce erroneous results. It is important not to misuse conversion factors when arranging hedge ratios.

CTD		5.75% 2009	Modified duration				7.234565567	
Conversion factor		0.9124950	Price				99.84	
Bond	Nominal amount (£m)	Price	Yield %	Duration	Modified duration	Relative volatility	Number of contracts
UKT 8% 2000	12	102.17	5.972	1.072	1.011587967	0.143090242	15.67
UKT 7% 2002	5	101.50	6.367	2.388	2.245057208	0.315483336	14.39
UKT 5% 2004	38	94.74	6.327	4.104	3.859791022	0.50626761	175.55
UKT 5.75% 2009	100	99.84	5.770	7.652	7.234565567	1.00	912.50
UKT 6% 2028	45	119.25	4.770	15.031	14.34666412	2.368603078	972.60
Total	200						2090.71

Table 3.3: Bond futures hedge for hypothetical gilt portfolio, 20 October 1999

bond. The bond with the highest volatility is not surprisingly the 6% 2028, which has the longest maturity of all the bonds and hence the highest modified duration. We note from Table 3.3 that the portfolio requires a hedge position of 2091 futures contracts. This illustrates how a "rough-and-ready" estimate of the hedging requirement, based on nominal values, would be insufficient as that would suggest a hedge position of only 2000 contracts.

The effectiveness of the hedge must be monitored over time. No hedge will be completely perfect however, and the calculation illustrated above, as it uses modified duration value, does not take into account the convexity effect of the bonds. The reason why a futures hedge will not be perfect is because in practice, the price of the futures contract will not move tick-for-tick with the CTD bond, at least not over a period of time. This is the basis risk that is inherent in hedging cash bonds with futures. In addition, the calculation of the hedge is only completely accurate for a parallel shift in yields, as it is based on modified duration, so as the yield curve changes around pivots, the hedge will move out of line. Finally, the long gilt future is not the appropriate contract to use to hedge three of the bonds in the portfolio, or over 25% of the portfolio by nominal value. This is because these bonds are short- or medium-dated, and so their price movements will not track the futures price as closely as longer-dated bonds. In this case, the more appropriate futures contract to use would have been the medium gilt contract, or (for the first bond, the 8% 2000) a strip of short sterling contracts. Using shorter-dated instruments would reduce some of the basis risk contained in the portfolio hedge.

35.4 The margin process

Institutions buying and selling futures on an exchange deal with only one counterparty at all times, the exchange clearing house. The clearing house is responsible for the settlement of all contracts, including managing the delivery process. A central clearing mechanism eliminates counterparty risk for anyone dealing on the exchange, because the clearing house guarantees the settlement of all transactions. The clearing house may be owned by the exchange itself, such as the one associated with the Chicago Mercantile Exchange (the CME Clearinghouse) or it may be a separate entity, such as the London Clearing House, which settles transactions on LIFFE. The LCH is also involved in running clearing systems for swaps and repo products in certain currencies.

One of the key benefits to the market of the clearing house mechanism is that counterparty risk, as it is transferred to the clearing house, is virtually eliminated. The mechanism that enables the clearing house to accept the counterparty risk is the *margining* process that is employed at all futures exchanges. A bank or local trader must deposit margin before commencing dealing on the exchange; each day a further amount must be deposited or will be returned, depending on the results of the day's trading activity.

The exchange will specify the level of margin that must be deposited for each type of futures contract that a bank wishes to deal in. The *initial margin* will be a fixed sum per lot, so for example if the margin was £1000 per lot an opening position of 100 lots would require a margin of £100,000. Once the initial margin has been deposited, there is a mark-to-market of all positions at the close of business; exchange-traded instruments are the most transparent products in the market, and the closing price is not only known to everyone, it is also indisputable. The closing price is also known as the *settlement price*. Any losses suffered by a trading counterparty, whether closed out or run overnight, are entered as a debit on the party's account and must be paid the next day. Trading profits are credited and may be withdrawn from the margin account the next day. This daily process is known as *variation margining*. Thus the margin account is updated on a daily basis and the maximum loss that must be made up on any morning is the maximum price movement that occurred the previous day. It is a serious issue if a trading party is unable to meet a margin call. In such a case, the exchange will order it to cease trading, and will also liquidate all its open positions; any losses will be met out of the firm's margin account. If the level of funds in the margin account is insufficient, the losses will be made good from funds paid out of a general fund run by the clearing house, which is maintained by all members of the exchange.

Payment of margin is made by electronic funds transfer between the trading party's bank account and the clearing house. Initial margin is usually paid in cash, although clearing houses will also accept high-quality securities such as T-bills or certain government bonds, to the value of the margin required. Variation margin is always cash. The advantage of depositing securities rather than cash is that the depositing firm earns interest on its margin. This is not available on a cash margin, and the interest foregone on a cash margin is effectively the cost of trading futures on the exchange. However if securities are used, there is effectively no cost associated with trading on the exchange (we ignore of course infrastructure costs and staff salaries).

The daily settlement of exchange-traded futures contracts, as opposed to when the contract expires or the position is closed out, is the main reason why futures prices are not equal to forward prices for long-dated instruments.

Appendix 3.1: The conversion factor for the long gilt future

Here we describe the process used for the calculation of the *conversion factor* or *price factor* for deliverable bonds of the long gilt contract. The contract specifies a bond of maturity

$8\frac{3}{4}$ 13 years and a notional coupon of 7%. For each bond that is eligible to be in the delivery basket, the conversion factor is given by the following equation: $P(7)/100$ where the numerator $P(7)$ is equal to the price per £100 nominal of the deliverable gilt at which it has a gross redemption yield of 7%, calculated as at the first day of the delivery month, less the accrued interest on the bond on that day. This calculation uses the formulae given in equation (A1.1.1) and the equation used to calculate accrued interest.

The numerator $P(7)$ is given by equation (A3.1.1):

$$p(7) = \frac{1}{1.035^{t/s}}\left(c_1 + \frac{c_2}{1.035} + \frac{C}{0.07}\left(\frac{1}{1.035} - \frac{1}{1.035^n}\right) + \frac{100}{1.035^n}\right) - AI \quad \text{(A3.1.1)}$$

where

c_1 is the cash flow due on the following quasi-coupon date, per £100 nominal of the gilt. c_1 will be zero if the first day of the delivery month occurs in the ex-dividend period or if the gilt has a long first coupon period and the first day of the delivery month occurs in the first full coupon period. c_1 will be less than c_2 if the first day of the delivery month falls in a short first coupon period. c_1 will be greater than c_2 if the first day of the delivery month falls in a long first coupon period and the first day of the delivery month occurs in the second full coupon period;

c_2 is the cash flow due on the next but one quasi-coupon date, per £100 nominal of the gilt. c_1 will be greater than c_2 if the first day of the delivery month falls in a long first coupon period and in the first full coupon period. In all other cases, $c_2 = C\backslash sol\ 2$; C is the annual coupon of the gilt, per £100 nominal;

t is the number of calendar days from and including the first day of the delivery month up to but excluding the next quasi-coupon date;

s is the number of calendar days in the full coupon period in which the first day of the delivery month occurs;

n is the number of full coupon periods between the following quasi-coupon date and the redemption date;

AI is the accrued interest per £100 nominal of the gilt.

The accrued interest used in the formula above is given according to the following procedures.

If the first day of the delivery month occurs in a standard coupon period, and the first day of the delivery month occurs on or before the ex-dividend date, then:

$$AI = \frac{t}{s} \times \frac{C}{2} \qquad\qquad (A3.1.2)$$

If the first day of the delivery month occurs in a standard coupon period, and the first day of the delivery month occurs after the ex-dividend date, then:

$$AI = \left(\frac{t}{s} - 1\right) \times \frac{C}{2} \qquad\qquad (A3.1.3)$$

where

t is the number of calendar days from and including the last coupon date up to but excluding the first day of the delivery month;

s is the number of calendar days in the full coupon period in which the first day of the delivery month occurs.

If the first day of the delivery month occurs in a short first coupon period, and the first day of the delivery month occurs on or before the ex-dividend date, then:

$$AI = \frac{t^*}{s} \times \frac{C}{2} \qquad\qquad (A3.1.4)$$

If the first day of the delivery month occurs in a short first coupon period, and the first day of the delivery month occurs after the ex-dividend date, then:

$$AI = \frac{t^* - n}{s} \times \frac{C}{2} \qquad\qquad (A5.1.5)$$

where

t^* is the number of calendar days from and including the issue date up to but excluding the first day of the delivery month;

n is the number of calendar days from and including the issue date up to but excluding the next quasi-coupon date.

If the first day of the delivery month occurs in a long first coupon period, and during the first full coupon period, then:

$$AI = \frac{u}{s_1} \times \frac{C}{2} \tag{A3.1.6}$$

If the first day of the delivery month occurs in a long first coupon period, and during the second full coupon period and on or before the ex-dividend date, then:

$$AI = \left(\frac{p_1}{s_1} + \frac{p_2}{s_2}\right) \times \frac{C}{2} \tag{A3.1.7}$$

If the first day of the delivery month occurs in a long first coupon period, and during the second full coupon period and after the ex-dividend date, then:

$$AI = \left(\frac{p_2}{s_2} - 1\right) \times \frac{C}{2} \tag{A3.1.8}$$

where

u is the number of calendar days from and including the issue date up to but excluding the first day of the delivery month;

$s1$ is the number of calendar days in the full coupon period in which the issue date occurs;

$s2$ is the number of days in the next full coupon period after the full coupon period in which the issue date occurs;

$p1$ is the number of calendar days from and including the issue date up to but excluding the next quasi-coupon date; $p2$ is the number of calendar days from and including the quasi-coupon date after the issue date up to but excluding the first day of the delivery month which falls in the next full coupon period after the full coupon period in which the issue date occurs.

Selected bibliography and references

Fabozzi, F., *Fixed Income Mathematics*, Probus 1993
Galitz, L., *Financial Engineering*, FT Pitman 1995
Kolb, R., *Futures, Options and Swaps*, Blackwell 2000

4 Interest-Rate Swaps

Swaps are off-balance sheet instruments involving combinations of two or more basic building blocks. Most swaps currently traded in the market involve combinations of cash market securities, for example a fixed interest rate security combined with a floating interest rate security, possibly also combined with a currency transaction. However the market has also seen swaps that involve a futures or forward component, as well as swaps that involve an option component. The market in say, dollar, euro and sterling interest rate swaps is very large and very liquid. The main types of swap are interest rate swaps, asset swaps, basis swaps, fixed-rate currency swaps and currency coupon swaps. The market for swaps is organised by the International Swap Dealers Association.

Swaps are now one of the most important and useful instruments in the debt capital markets. They are used by a wide range of institutions, including banks, mortgage banks and building societies, corporates and local authorities. The demand for them has grown as the continuing uncertainty and volatility of interest rates and exchange rates has made it ever more important to hedge their exposures. As the market has matured the instrument has gained wider acceptance, and is regarded as a "plain vanilla" product in the debt capital markets. Virtually all commercial and investment banks will quote swap prices for their customers, and as they are OTC instruments, dealt over the telephone, it is possible for banks to tailor swaps to match the precise requirements of individual customers. There is also a close relationship between the bond market and the swap market, and corporate finance teams and underwriting banks keep a close eye on the government yield curve and the swap yield curve, looking out for possibilities regarding new issue of debt.

It is not proposed to cover the historical evolution of the swaps market, which is abundantly covered in existing literature, nor the myriad of swap products which can be traded today. In this chapter we review the use of interest rate swaps from the point of view of the bond market participant; this includes pricing and valuation and its use as a hedging tool. The bibliography lists further reading on important topics such as pricing, valuation and credit risk.[1]

4.1 Interest rate swaps

4.1.1 Introduction

Interest rate swaps are the most important type of swap in terms of volume of transactions. They are used to manage and hedge interest rate risk and exposure,

---

[1]   This chapter is abridged from Choudhry (2001), Chapter 11.

while market makers will also take positions in swaps that reflect their view on the direction of interest rates. An interest rate swap is an agreement between two counterparties to make periodic interest payments to one another during the life of the swap, on a predetermined set of dates, based on a *notional* principal amount. One party is the fixed-rate payer, and this rate is agreed at the time of trade of the swap; the other party is the floating-rate payer, the floating rate being determined during the life of the swap by reference to a specific market index. The principal or notional amount is never physically exchanged, hence the term "off-balance sheet", but is used merely to calculate the interest payments. The fixed-rate payer receives floating-rate interest and is said to be "long" or to have "bought" the swap. The long side has conceptually purchased a floating-rate note (because it receives floating-rate interest) and issued a fixed coupon bond (because it pays out fixed interest at intervals), that is, it has in principle borrowed funds. The floating-rate payer is said to be "short" or to have "sold" the swap. The short side has conceptually purchased a coupon bond (because it receives fixed-rate interest) and issued a floating-rate note (because it pays floating-rate interest). So an interest rate swap is:

- an agreement between two parties
- to exchange a stream of cash flows
- calculated as a percentage of a *notional* sum
- and calculated on different interest bases.

For example in a trade between Bank A and Bank B, Bank A may agree to pay fixed semi-annual coupons of 10% on a notional principal sum of £1 million, in return for receiving from Bank B the prevailing six-month sterling LIBOR rate on the same amount. The known cash flow is the fixed payment of £50,000 every six months by Bank A to Bank B.

Interest rate swaps trade in a secondary market so their value moves in line with market interest rates, in exactly the same way as bonds. If a five-year interest rate swap is transacted today at a rate of 5%, and five-year interest rates subsequently fall to 4.75%, the swap will have decreased in value to the fixed-rate payer, and correspondingly increased in value to the floating-rate payer, who has now seen the level of interest payments fall. The opposite would be true if five-year rates moved to 5.25%. Why is this? Consider the fixed-rate payer in an IR swap to be a borrower of funds; if she fixes the interest rate payable on a loan for five years, and then this interest rate decreases shortly afterwards, is she better off? No, because she is now paying above the market rate for the funds borrowed. For this reason a swap contract decreases in value to the fixed-rate payer if there is a fall in rates. Equally a floating-rate payer gains if there is a fall in rates, as he can take advantage of the new rates and pay a lower level of interest; hence the value of a swap increases to the floating-rate payer if there is a fall in rates.

A bank swaps desk will have an overall net interest rate position arising from all the swaps it has traded that are currently on the book. This position is an interest rate exposure at all points along the term structure, out to the maturity of the longest-dated swap. At the close of business each day all the swaps on the book will be *marked-to-market* at the interest rate quote for that day.

A swap can be viewed in two ways, either as a bundle of forward or futures contracts, or as a bundle of cash flows arising from the "sale" and "purchase" of cash market instruments. If we imagine a strip of futures contracts, maturing every three or six months out to three years, we can see how this is conceptually similar to a three-year interest rate swap. However in the author's view it is better to visualise a swap as being a bundle of cash flows arising from cash instruments.

Let us imagine we have only two positions on our book:

- a long position in £100 million of a three-year FRN that pays six-month LIBOR semi-annually, and is trading at par;
- a short position in £100 million of a three-year gilt with coupon of 6% that is also trading at par.

Being short a bond is the equivalent to being a borrower of funds. Assuming this position is kept to maturity, the resulting cash flows are shown in Table 4.1.

There is no net outflow or inflow at the start of these trades, as the £100 million purchase of the FRN is netted with receipt of £100 million from the sale of the gilt. The resulting cash flows over the three-year period are shown in the last column of Table 4.1. This net position is exactly the same as that of a fixed-rate payer in an IR swap. As we had at the start of the trade, there is no cash inflow or outflow on maturity. For a floating-rate payer, the cash flow would mirror exactly a long position in a fixed-rate bond and a short position in an FRN. Therefore the fixed-rate payer in a swap is said to be short in the bond market, that is a borrower of funds; the floating-rate payer in a swap is said to be long in the bond market.

Cashflows resulting from long position in FRN and short position in gilt

Period (6 mo)	FRN	Gilt	Net cash flow
0	−£100 m	+£100 m	£0
1	+(LIBOR × 100)/2	−3	+(LIBOR × 100)/2 − 3.0
2	+(LIBOR × 100)/2	−3	+(LIBOR × 100)/2 − 3.0
3	+(LIBOR × 100)/2	−3	+(LIBOR × 100)/2 − 3.0
4	+(LIBOR × 100)/2	−3	+(LIBOR × 100)/2 − 3.0
5	+(LIBOR × 100)/2	−3	+(LIBOR × 100)/2 − 3.0
6	+[(LIBOR × 100)/2] + 100	−103	+(LIBOR × 100)/2 − 3.0

Table 4.1: Three-year cash flows. The LIBOR rate is the six-month rate prevailing at the time of the setting, for instance the LIBOR rate at period 4 will be the rate actually prevailing at period 4

4.1.2 Market terminology

Virtually all swaps are traded under the legal terms and conditions stipulated in the ISDA standard documentation. The trade date for a swap is, not surprisingly, the date on which the swap is transacted. The terms of the trade include the fixed interest rate, the maturity and notional amount of the swap, and the payment bases of both legs of the swap. The date from which floating interest payments are determined is the *setting date*, which may also be the trade date. Most swaps fix the floating-rate payments to LIBOR, although other reference rates that are used include the US prime rate, euribor, the Treasury bill rate and the commercial paper rate. In the same way as for FRA and eurocurrency deposits, the rate is fixed two business days before the interest period begins. The second (and subsequent) setting date will be two business days before the beginning of the second (and subsequent) swap periods. The *effective date* is the date from which interest on the swap is calculated, and this is typically two business days after the trade date. In a *forward*-start swap the effective date will be at some point in the future, specified in the swap terms. The floating interest rate for each period is fixed at the start of the period, so that the interest payment amount is known in advance by both parties (the fixed rate is known of course, throughout the swap by both parties).

Although for the purposes of explaining swap structures, both parties are said to pay interest payments (and receive them), in practice only the net difference between both payments changes hands at the end of each interest period. This eases the administration associated with swaps and reduces the number of cash flows for each swap. The counterparty that is the net payer at the end of each period will make a payment to the counterparty. The first payment date will occur at the end of the first interest period, and subsequent payment dates will fall at the end of successive interest periods. The final payment date falls on the maturity date of the swap. The calculation of interest is given by equation (4.1).

$$I = M \times r \times \frac{n}{B} \qquad\qquad (4.1)$$

where

I   is the interest amount;
M   is the nominal amount of the swap;
B   is the interest day-base for the swap.

Dollar and euro-denominated swaps use an actual/360 day count, similar to other money market instruments in those currencies, while sterling swaps use an actual/365 day count basis.

The cash flows resulting from a vanilla interest rate swap are illustrated in Figure 4.1, using the normal convention where cash inflows are shown as an arrow pointing up, while cash outflows are shown as an arrow pointing down. The counterparties in a swap transaction only pay across net cash flows however, so at

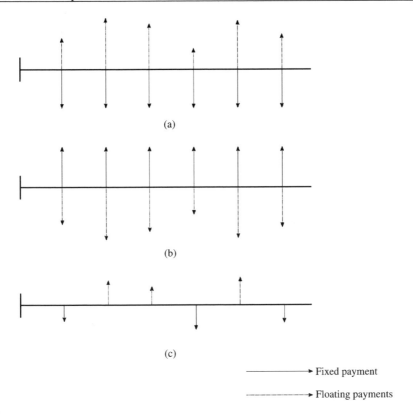

Figure 4.1: Cash flows for typical interest rate swap. (a) Cash flows for fixed-rate payer. (b) Cash flows for floating-rate payer. (c) Net cash flows

each interest payment date only one actual cash transfer will be made, by the net payer. This is shown as Figure 4.1(c).

4.1.3 Swap spreads and the swap yield curve

In the market banks will quote two-way swap rates, on screens and on the telephone or via a dealing system such as Reuters. Brokers will also be active in relaying prices in the market. The convention in the market is for the swap market maker to set the floating leg at LIBOR and then quote the fixed rate that is payable for that maturity. So for a five-year swap a bank's swap desk might be willing to quote the following:

Floating-rate payer:	pay 6 mo LIBOR
	receive fixed rate of 5.19%
Fixed-rate payer:	pay fixed rate of 5.25%
	receive 6 mo LIBOR

1 year	4.50	4.45	+17
2 years	4.69	4.62	+25
3 years	4.88	4.80	+23
4 years	5.15	5.05	+29
5 years	5.25	5.19	+31
10 years	5.50	5.40	+35

Table 4.2: Swap quotes

In this case the bank is quoting an offer rate of 5.25%, which the fixed-rate payer will pay, in return for receiving LIBOR flat. The bid price quote is 5.19% which is what a floating-rate payer will receive fixed. The bid–offer spread in this case is therefore 6 basis points. The fixed-rate quotes are always at a spread above the government bond yield curve. Let us assume that the five-year gilt is yielding 4.88%; in this case then the five-year swap bid rate is 31 basis points above this yield. So the bank's swap trader could quote the swap rates as a spread above the benchmark bond yield curve, say 37 − 31, which is her swap spread quote. This means that the bank is happy to enter into a swap paying fixed 31 basis points above the benchmark yield and receiving LIBOR, and receiving fixed 37 basis points above the yield curve and paying LIBOR. The banks screen on say, Bloomberg or Reuters might look something like Table 4.2, which quotes the swap rates as well as the current spread over the government bond benchmark.

The swap spread is a function of the same factors that influence the spread over government bonds for other instruments. For shorter duration swaps, say up to three years, there are other yield curves that can be used in comparison, such as the cash market curve or a curve derived from futures prices. For longer-dated swaps the spread is determined mainly by the credit spreads that prevail in the corporate bond market. Because a swap is viewed as a package of long and short positions in fixed- and floating-rate bonds, it is the credit spreads in these two markets that will determine the swap spread. This is logical; essentially it is the premium for greater credit risk involved in lending to corporates that dictates that a swap rate will be higher than the same maturity government bond yield. Technical factors will be responsible for day-to-day fluctuations in swap rates, such as the supply of corporate bonds and the level of demand for swaps, plus the cost to swap traders of hedging their swap positions.

We can summarise by saying that swap spreads over government bonds reflect the supply and demand conditions of both swaps and government bonds, as well as the market's view on the credit quality of swap counterparties. There is considerable information content in the swap yield curve, much like that in the government bond yield curve. During times of credit concerns in the market, such as the corrections in Asian and Latin American markets in summer 1998, and the possibility of default by the Russian government regarding its long-dated US dollar bonds, the swap spread will increase, more so at higher maturities. To illustrate

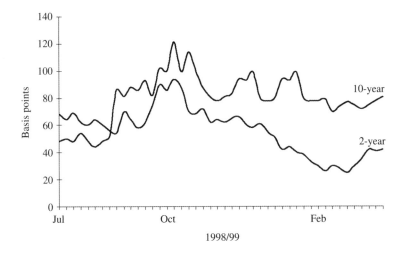

Figure 6.2: Sterling 2-year and 10-year swap spreads 1998/99

this let us consider the sterling swap spread in 1998/99. The UK swap spread widened from the second half of 1998 onwards, a reaction to bond market volatility around the world. At such times investors embark on a "flight to quality" that results in yield spreads widening. In the swap market, the spread between two-year and ten-year swaps also increased, reflecting market concern with credit and counterparty risk. The spreads narrowed in the first quarter 1999, as credit concerns brought about by market corrections in 1998 declined. The change in swap spreads is shown in Figure 4.2.

4.2 Generic swap valuation

Banks generally use *par* swap or *zero-coupon* swap pricing. We will look at this method in Section 4.2.2; first however we will introduce an intuitive swap valuation method.

46.2.1 Generic swap pricing

Assume we have a vanilla interest rate swap with a notional principal of N that pays n payments during its life, to a maturity date of T. The date of each payment is on t_i with $i = 1, \ldots, n$. The present value today of a future payment is denoted by $PV(0, t)$. If the swap rate is r, the value of the fixed-leg payments is given by equation (4.2) below:

$$PV_{fixed} = N \sum_{i=1}^{n} PV(0, t_i) \times \left[r \times \left(\frac{t_i - t_{i-1}}{B} \right) \right] \qquad (4.2)$$

where B is the money market day base. The term $t_i - t_{i-1}$ is simply the number of days between the ith and the $i-1$th payments.

The value of the floating-leg payments at the date $t1$ for an existing swap is given by:

$$PV_{float} = N \times \left[rl \times \frac{t_1}{B} \right] + N - [N \times PV(t_1, t_n)] \tag{4.3}$$

where rl is the LIBOR rate that has been set for the next interest payment. We set the present value of the floating-rate payment at time 0 as follows:

$$PV(0, t_1) = \frac{1}{1 + rl(t_1)\left(\dfrac{t_1}{B}\right)} \tag{4.4}$$

For a new swap the value of the floating payments is given by:

$$PV_{float} = N \left[rl \times \frac{t_1}{B} + 1 \right] \times PV(0, t_1) - PV(0, t_n) \tag{4.5}$$

The swap valuation is then given by $PV_{fixed} - PV_{float}$. The swap rate quoted by a market making bank is that which sets $PV_{fixed} = PV_{float}$ and is known as the par or zero-coupon swap rate. We consider this next.

4.2.2 Zero-coupon swap pricing

So far we have discussed how vanilla swap prices are often quoted as a spread over the benchmark government bond yield in that currency, and how this swap spread is mainly a function of the credit spread required by the market over the government (risk-free) rate. This method is convenient and also logical because banks use government bonds as the main instrument when hedging their swap books. However because much bank swap trading is now conducted in non-standard, tailor-made swaps, this method can sometimes be unwieldy as each swap needs to have its spread calculated to suit its particular characteristics. Therefore banks use a standard pricing method for all swaps known as *zero-coupon* swap pricing.

In Chapter 2 we referred to zero-coupon bonds and zero-coupon interest rates. Zero-coupon rates, or *spot rates* are true interest rates for their particular term to maturity. In zero-coupon swap pricing, a bank will view all swaps, even the most complex, as a series of cash flows. The zero-coupon rates that apply now for each of the cash flows in a swap can be used to value these cash flows. Therefore to value and price a swap, each of the swap's cash flows are present valued using known spot rates; the sum of these present values is the value of the swap.

In a swap the fixed-rate payments are known in advance and so it is straightforward to present value them. The present value of the floating-rate payments is usually estimated in two stages. First the implied forward rates can be calculated using equation (6.6). We are quite familiar with this relationship from our reading of the earlier chapter.

$$rf_i = \left(\frac{df_i}{df_{i+1}} - 1\right)N \qquad (4.6)$$

where

rf_i is the one-period forward rate starting at time i;
df_i is the discount factor for the maturity period I;
df_{i+1} is the discount factor for the period $i+1$;
N is the number of times per year that coupons are paid.

By definition the floating-payment interest rates are not known in advance, so the swap bank will predict what these will be, using the forward rates applicable to each payment date. The forward rates are those that are currently implied from spot rates. Once the size of the floating-rate payments has been estimated, these can also be valued by using the spot rates. The total value of the fixed and floating legs is the sum of all the present values, so the value of the total swap is the net of the present values of the fixed and floating legs.

While the term *zero-coupon* refers to an interest rate that applies to a discount instrument that pays no coupon and has one cash flow (at maturity), it is not necessary to have a functioning zero-coupon bond market in order to construct a zero-coupon yield curve. In practice most financial pricing models use a combination of the following instruments to construct zero-coupon yield curves:

■ money market deposits;
■ interest rate futures;
■ Forward Rate Agreements or FRAs;
■ government bonds.

Frequently an overlap in the maturity period of all instruments is used; FRA rates are usually calculated from interest rate futures so it is necessary to use only one of either FRA or futures rates.

Once a zero-coupon yield curve (*term structure*) is derived, this may be used to value a future cash flow maturing at any time along the term structure. This includes swaps: to price an interest rate swap, we calculate the present value of each of the cash flows using the zero-coupon rates and then sum all the cash flows. As we noted above, while the fixed-rate payments are known in advance, the floating-rate payments must be estimated, using the forward rates implied by the zero-coupon yield curve. The net present value of the swap is the net difference between the present values of the fixed- and floating-rate legs.

4.2.3 Calculating the forward rate from the spot rate discount factors

Remember that one way to view a swap is as a long position in a fixed-coupon bond that was funded at LIBOR, or against a short position in a floating-rate bond. The cash flows from such an arrangement would be paying floating rate and receiving fixed rate. In the former arrangement, where a long position in a fixed-rate bond is funded with a floating-rate loan, the cash flows from the principals will cancel out, as they are equal and opposite (assuming the price of the bond on purchase was par), leaving a collection of cash flows that mirror an interest rate swap that pays floating and receives fixed. Therefore, as the fixed rate on an interest rate swap is the same as the coupon (and yield) on a bond priced at par, calculating the fixed rate on an interest rate swap is the same as calculating the coupon for a bond that we wish to issue at par.

The price of a bond paying semi-annual coupons is given by equation (4.7), which may be rearranged for the coupon rate r to provide an equation that enables us to determine the par yield, and hence the swap rate r, given by equation (4.8):

$$P = \frac{r_n}{2} df_1 + \frac{r_n}{2} df_2 + \ldots + \frac{r_n}{2} df_n + M df_n \qquad (4.7)$$

where r_n is the coupon on an n-period bond with n coupons and M is the maturity payment. It can be shown then that

$$
\begin{aligned}
r_n &= \frac{1 - df_n}{\dfrac{df_1}{2} + \dfrac{df_2}{2} + \ldots + \dfrac{df_n}{2}} \\
&= \frac{1 - df_n}{\displaystyle\sum_{i=1}^{n} \frac{df_i}{2}}
\end{aligned}
\qquad (4.8)
$$

For annual coupon bonds there is no denominator for the discount factor, while for bonds paying coupons on a frequency of N we replace the denominator 2 with N.[2] Equation (4.8) may be rearranged again, using F for the coupon frequency, to obtain an equation which may be used to calculate the nth discount factor for an n-period swap rate, given as equation (4.9):

$$df_n = \frac{1 - r_n \displaystyle\sum_{i=1}^{n-1} \frac{df_i}{N}}{1 + \dfrac{r_n}{N}} \qquad (4.9)$$

Equation (4.9) is the general equation for the *boot-strapping* process of

---

[2]   The equation also assumes an actual/365 day count basis. If any other day count convention isused, the $1/N$ factor must be replaced by a fraction made up of the actual number of days as the numerator and the appropriate year base as the denominator.

constructing a zero-coupon curve. Essentially, to calculate the n-year discount factor we use the discount factors for the years 1 to $n-1$, and the n-year swap rate or zero-coupon rate. If we have the discount factor for any period, we may use equation (4.9) to determine the same period zero-coupon rate, after rearranging it, shown as equation (4.10):

$$rs_n = t_n \sqrt{\frac{1}{df_n} - 1} \qquad (4.10)$$

Discount factors for spot rates may also be used to calculate forward rates. We know that

$$df_1 = \frac{1}{\left(1 + \dfrac{rs_1}{N}\right)} \qquad (4.11)$$

where rs is the zero-coupon rate. If we know the *forward rate* we may use this to calculate a second discount rate, shown by equation (4.12):

$$df_2 = \frac{df_1}{\left(1 + \dfrac{rf_1}{N}\right)} \qquad (4.12)$$

where rf_1 is the forward rate. This is no use in itself, however we may derive from it an equation to enable us to calculate the discount factor at any point in time between the previous discount rate and the given forward rate for the period n to $n+1$, shown as equation (4.13), which may then be rearranged to give us the general equation to calculate a forward rate, given as equation (4.14).

$$df_{n+1} = \frac{df_n}{\left(1 + \dfrac{rf_n}{N}\right)} \qquad (4.13)$$

$$rf_n = \left(\frac{df_n}{df_{n+1}} - 1\right) N \qquad (4.14)$$

The general equation for an n-period discount rate at time n from the previous period forward rates is given by equation (4.15).

$$df_n = \frac{1}{\left(1 + \dfrac{rf_{n-1}}{N}\right)} \times \frac{1}{\left(1 + \dfrac{rf_{n-2}}{N}\right)} \times \ldots \times \frac{1}{\left(1 + \dfrac{rf_n}{N}\right)}$$

$$ \qquad (4.15)$$

$$df_n = \prod_{i=0}^{n-1} \left[\frac{1}{\left(1 + \dfrac{rf_i}{N}\right)}\right]$$

From the above we may combine equations (4.8) and (4.14) to obtain the general expression for an n-period swap rate and zero-coupon rate, given by equations (4.16) and (4.17) respectively.

$$r_n = \frac{\displaystyle\sum_{i=1}^{n} \frac{rf_{i-1} \, df_i}{N}}{\displaystyle\sum_{i=1}^{n} \frac{df_i}{F}} \tag{4.16}$$

$$1 + rs_n = t_n \sqrt[n-1]{\prod_{i=0}^{n-1} \left(1 + \frac{rf_i}{N}\right)} \tag{4.17}$$

The swap rate, which we have denoted as r_n is shown by equation (4.16) to be the weighted average of the forward rates. Consider that a strip of FRAs would constitute an interest rate swap, that is a swap rate for a continuous period could be covered by a strip of FRAs. Therefore an average of the FRA rates would be the correct swap rate. As FRA rates are forward rates, we may be comfortable with equation (4.16), which states that the n-period swap rate is the average of the forward rates from rf_0 to rf_n. To be accurate we must weight the forward rates, and these are weighted by the discount factors for each period. Note that although swap rates are derived from forward rates, interest payments under a swap are paid in the normal way at the end of an interest period, while payments for an FRA are made at the beginning of the period and must be discounted.

Equation (4.17) states that the zero-coupon rate is calculated from the geometric average of (one plus) the forward rates. The n-period forward rate is obtained using the discount factors for periods n and $n-1$. The discount factor for the complete period is obtained by multiplying the individual discount factors together, and exactly the same result would be obtained by using the zero-coupon interest rate for the whole period to obtain the discount factor.[3]

4.2.4 Illustrating the principles for an interest rate swap

The rate charged on a newly-transacted interest rate swap is the one that gives its net present value as zero. The term *valuation* of a swap is used to denote the process of calculating the net present value of an existing swap, when marking-to-market the swap against current market interest rates. Therefore when we price a

---

[3] Zero-coupon and forward rates are also related in another way. If we change the zero-coupon rate rs_n and the forward rate rf_i into their continuously compounded equivalent rates, given by $\ln(1 + rs_n)$ and the $\ln(1 + rf_i)$, we may obtain an equation for the continuously compounded zero-coupon rate as being the simple average of the continuously compounded forward rates, given by:

$$rs'_n = \frac{1}{t_n} \sum_{i=0}^{n-1} \frac{rf'_i}{F}.$$

swap, we set its net present value to zero, while when we value a swap we set its fixed rate at the market rate and calculate the net present value.

To illustrate the basic principle, we price a plain vanilla interest rate swap with the terms set out below; for simplicity we assume that the annual fixed-rate payments are the same amount each year, although in practice there would be slight differences. Also assume we already have our zero-coupon yields as shown in Table 4.3.

We use the zero-coupon rates to calculate the discount factors, and then use the discount factors to calculate the forward rates. This is done using equation (4.14). These forward rates are then used to predict what the floating-rate payments will be at each interest period. Both fixed-rate and floating-rate payments are then present valued at the appropriate zero-coupon rate, which enables us to calculate the net present value.

The fixed rate for the swap is calculated using equation (4.8) to give us:

$$\frac{1 - 0.71298618}{4.16187950}$$

or 6.8963%.

Nominal principal	£10,000,000
Fixed rate	6.8963%
Day count fixed	Actual/365
Day count floating	Actual/365
Payment frequency fixed	Annual
Payment frequency floating	Annual
Trade date	31 January 2000
Effective date	2 February 2000
Maturity date	2 February 2005
Term	Five years

For reference the Microsoft Excel® formulae are shown in Table 4.4. It is not surprising that the net present value is zero, because the zero-coupon curve is used to derive the discount factors which are then used to derive the forward rates, which are used to value the swap. As with any financial instrument, the fair value is its breakeven price or hedge cost, and in this case the bank that is pricing the five-year swap shown in Table 4.3 could hedge the swap with a series of FRAs transacted at the forward rates shown. If the bank is paying fixed and receiving floating, the value of the swap to it will rise if there is a rise in market rates, and fall if there is a fall in market rates. Conversely, if the bank was receiving fixed and paying floating, the swap value to it would fall if there was a rise in rates, and vice versa.

This method is used to price any interest rate swap, even exotic ones.

Period	Zero-coupon rate %	Discount factor	Forward rate %	Fixed payment	Floating payment	PV fixed payment	PV floating payment
1	5.5	0.947867298	5.5	689,625	550000	653672.9858	521327.0142
2	6	0.88999644	6.502369605	689,625	650236.9605	613763.7949	578708.58
3	6.25	0.833706493	6.751770257	689,625	675177.0257	574944.8402	562899.4702
4	6.5	0.777323091	7.253534951	689,625	725353.4951	536061.4366	563834.0208
5	7	0.712986179	9.023584719	689,625	902358.4719	491693.094	643369.1194
		4.161879501				2870137	2870137

Table 4.3: Generic interest rate swap

CELL	C	D	E	F	G	H	I	J
21			10000000					
22								
23		Period	Zero-coupon rate %	Discount factor	Forward rate %	Fixed payment	Floating payment	PV fixed payment	PV floating payment
24	1	5.5	0.947867298	5.5	689,625	"(F24*10000000)/100	"G24/1.055	"H24/(1.055)
25	2	6	0.88999644	"((E24/E25) − 1)*100	689,625	"(F25*10000000)/100	"G24/(1.06)1^2	"H25/(1.06)1^2
26	3	6.25	0.833706493	"((E25/E26) − 1)*100	689,625	"(F26*10000000)/100	"G24/(1.0625)1^3	"H26/(1.0625)p1^3
27	4	6.5	0.777323091	"((E26/E27) − 1)*100	689,625	"(F27*10000000)/100	"G24/(1.065)1^4	"H27/(1.065)1^4
28	5	7	0.712986179	"((E27/E28) − 1)*100	689,625	"(F28*10000000)/100	"G24/(1.07)1^5	"H28/(1.07)1^5
			"SUM(E24:E28)				2,870,137	2,870,137

Table 4.4: Generic interest rate swap (Excel formulae)

4.2.5 Valuation using final maturity discount factor

A short-cut to valuing the floating-leg payments of an interest rate swap involves using the discount factor for the final maturity period. This is possible because, for the purposes of valuation, an exchange of principal at the beginning and end of the swap is conceptually the same as the floating-leg interest payments. This holds because, in an exchange of principal, the interest payments earned on investing the initial principal would be uncertain, as they are floating rate, while on maturity the original principal would be returned. The net result is a floating-rate level of receipts, exactly similar to the floating-leg payments in a swap. To value the principals then, we need only the final maturity discount rate.

To illustrate, consider Table 4.3, where the present value of both legs was found to be £2,870,137. The same result is obtained if we use the five-year discount factor, as shown below:

$$PV_{floating} = (10,000,000 \times 1) - (10,000,000 \times 0.71298618) = 2,870,137.$$

The first term is the principal multiplied by the discount factor 1; this is because the present value of an amount valued immediately is unchanged (or rather, it is multiplied by the immediate payment discount factor, which is 1.0000).

Therefore we may use the principal amount of a swap if we wish to value the swap. This is of course for valuation only, as there is no actual exchange of principal in a swap.

4.2.6 Summary of IR swap

Let us summarise the chief characteristics of swaps. A plain vanilla swap has the following characteristics: one leg of the swap is fixed-rate interest, while the other will be floating-rate, usually linked to a standard index such as LIBOR;

- the fixed rate is fixed through the entire life of the swap;
- the floating rate is set in advance of each period (quarterly, semi-annually or annually) and paid in arrears;
- both legs have the same payment frequency;
- the maturity can be standard whole years up to 30 years, or set to match customer requirements;
- the notional principal remains constant during the life of the swap.

Of course to meet customer demand banks can set up swaps that have variations on any or all of the above standard points. Some of the more common variations are discussed in Section 4.3.

4.3 Non-vanilla interest rate swaps

The swap market is very flexible and instruments can be tailor-made to fit the requirements of individual customers. A wide variety of swap contracts have been traded in the market. Although the most common reference rate for the floating leg of a swap is six-month LIBOR, for a semi-annual paying floating leg, other reference rates that have been used include three-month LIBOR, the prime rate (for dollar swaps), the one-month commercial paper rate, the Treasury bill rate and the municipal bond rate (again, for dollar swaps). The term of a swap need not be fixed; swaps may be *extendable* or *putable*. In an extendable swap, one of the parties has the right but not the obligation to extend the life of the swap beyond the fixed maturity date, while in a putable swap one party has the right to terminate the swap ahead of the specified maturity date. It is also possible to transact options on swaps, known as *swaptions*. A swaption is the right to enter into a swap agreement at some point in the future, during the life of the option. Essentially a swaption is an option to exchange a fixed-rate bond cash flow for a floating-rate bond cash flow structure. As a floating-rate bond is valued on its principal value at the start of a swap, a swaption may be viewed as the value on a fixed-rate bond, with a strike price that is equal to the face value of the floating-rate bond.

- A *constant maturity swap* is a swap in which the parties exchange a LIBOR rate for a fixed swap rate. For example, the terms of the swap might state that six-month LIBOR is exchanged for the five-year swap rate on a semi-annual basis for the next five years, or for the five-year government bond rate. In the US market the second type of constant maturity swap is known as a *constant maturity Treasury swap*.
- *Accreting and amortising swaps.* In a plain vanilla swap the notional principal remains unchanged during the life of the swap. However it is possible to trade a swap where the notional principal varies during its life. An accreting (or *step-up*) swap is one in which the principal starts off at one level and then increases in amount over time. The opposite, an amortising swap, is one in which the notional reduces in size over time. An accreting swap would be useful where, for instance a funding liability that is being hedged increases over time. The amortising swap might be employed by a borrower hedging a bond issue that featured sinking fund payments, where a part of the notional amount outstanding is paid off at set points during the life of the bond. If the principal fluctuates in amount, for example increasing in one year and then reducing in another, the swap is known as a *roller-coaster swap*. Another application for an amortising swap is as a hedge for a loan that is itself an amortising one. Frequently this is combined with a forward-starting swap, to tie in with the cash flows payable on the loan. The pricing and valuation of an amortising swap is no different in principle to a vanilla interest rate swap; a single swap rate is calculated using the relevant discount factors, and at this rate the net present value of the swap cash flows will equal zero at the start of the swap.

- *LIBOR-in-arrears swap.* In this type of swap (also known as a *back-set swap*) the setting date is just before the end of the accrual period for the floating rate setting and not just before the start. Such a swap would be attractive to a counterparty who had a different view on interest rates compared to the market consensus. For instance in a rising yield curve environment, forward rates will be higher than current market rates, and this will be reflected in the pricing of a swap. A LIBOR-in-arrears swap would be priced higher than a conventional swap. If the floating-rate payer believed that interest rates would in fact rise more slowly than forward rates (and the market) were suggesting, she may wish to enter into an arrears swap as opposed to a conventional swap.

- *Basis swap.* In a conventional swap one leg comprises fixed-rate payments and the other floating-rate payments. In a basis swap both legs are floating rate, but linked to different money market indices. One leg is normally linked to LIBOR, while the other might be linked to the CD rate say, or the commercial paper rate. This type of swap would be used by a bank in the US that had made loans that paid at the prime rate, and financed its loans at LIBOR. A basis swap would eliminate the *basis risk* between the bank's income and expense cash flows. Other basis swaps have been traded where both legs are linked to LIBOR, but at different maturities; for instance one leg might be at three-month LIBOR and the other at six-month LIBOR. In such a swap the basis is different and so is the payment frequency: one leg pays out semi-annually while the other would be paying on a quarterly basis. Note that where the payment frequencies differ, there is a higher level of counterparty risk for one of the parties. For instance, if one party is paying out on a monthly basis but receiving semi-annual cash flows, it would have made five interest payments before receiving one in return.

- *Margin swap.* It is common to encounter swaps where there is a margin above or below LIBOR on the floating leg, as opposed to a floating leg of LIBOR flat. If a bank's borrowing is financed at LIBOR + 25 bps, it may wish to receive LIBOR + 25 bps in the swap so that its cash flows match exactly. The fixed-rate quote for a swap must be adjusted correspondingly to allow for the margin on the floating side, so in our example if the fixed-rate quote is say, 6.00%, it would be adjusted to around 6.25%; differences in the margin quoted on the fixed leg might arise if the day count convention or payment frequency were to differ between fixed and floating legs. Another reason why there may be a margin is if the credit quality of the counterparty demanded it, so that highly rated counterparties may pay slightly below LIBOR, for instance.

- *Off-market swap.* When a swap is transacted its fixed rate is quoted at the current market rate for that maturity. Where the fixed rate is different to the market rate, this is an off-market swap, and a compensating payment is made by one party to the other. An off-market rate may be used for particular hedging requirements for example, or when a bond issuer wishes to use the swap to hedge the bond as well as to cover the bond's issue costs.

- *Differential swap*. A differential swap is a basis swap but with one of the legs calculated in a different currency. Typically one leg is floating rate, while the other is floating rate but with the reference index rate for another currency, but denominated in the domestic currency. For example, a differential swap may have one party paying six-month sterling LIBOR, in sterling, on a notional principal of £10 million, and receiving euro-LIBOR, minus a margin, payable in sterling and on the same notional principal. Differential swaps are not very common and are the most difficult for a bank to hedge. The hedging is usually carried out using what is known as a *quanto* option.
- *Forward-start swap*. A forward-start swap is one where the *effective date* is not the usual one or two days after the trade date but a considerable time afterwards, for instance say six months after trade date. Such a swap might be entered into where one counterparty wanted to fix a hedge or cost of borrowing now, but for a point some time in the future. Typically this would be because the party considered that interest rates would rise or the cost of hedging would rise. The swap rate for a forward-starting swap is calculated in the same way as that for a vanilla swap.

4.4   Currency swaps

So far we have discussed swap contracts where the interest payments are both in the same currency. A *cross-currency* swap, or simply *currency swap*, is similar to an interest rate swap, except that the currencies of the two legs are different. Like interest rate swaps, the legs are usually fixed and floating rate, although again it is common to encounter both fixed-rate or both floating-rate legs in a currency swap. On maturity of the swap there is an exchange of principals, and usually (but not always) there is an exchange of principals at the start of the swap. Where currencies are exchanged at the start of the swap, at the prevailing spot exchange rate for the two currencies, the exact amounts are exchanged back on maturity. During the time of the swap, the parties make interest payments in the currency that they have *received* where principals are exchanged. It may seem that exchanging the same amount on maturity gives rise to some sort of currency risk, in fact it is this feature that removes any element of currency risk from the swap transaction.

Currency swaps are widely used in association with bond issues by borrowers who seek to tap opportunities in different markets but have no requirement for that market's currency. By means of a currency swap, a company can raise funds in virtually any market and swap the proceeds into the currency that it requires. Often the underwriting bank that is responsible for the bond issue will also arrange for the currency swap to be transacted. In a currency swap therefore, the exchange of principal means that the value of the principal amounts must be accounted for, and is dependent on the prevailing spot exchange rate between the two currencies.

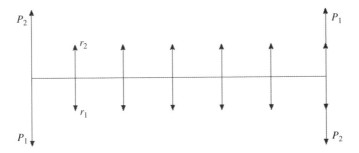

Figure 4.3: Fixed–fixed rate currency swap

4.4.1 Valuation of currency swaps

The same principles we established for the pricing and valuation of interest rate swaps may be applied to currency swaps. A generic currency swap with fixed-rate payment legs would be valued at the fair value swap rate for each currency, which would give a net present value of zero. The cash flows are illustrated in Figure 4.3. This shows that the two swap rates in a fixed–fixed currency swap would be identical to the same-maturity swap rate for each currency interest rate swap. So the swap rates for a fixed–fixed five-year sterling/dollar currency swap would be the five-year sterling swap rate and the five-year dollar swap rate.

A floating–floating currency swap may be valued in the same way, and for valuation purposes the floating-leg payments are replaced with an exchange of principals, as we observed for the floating leg of an interest rate swap. A fixed–floating currency swap is therefore valued at the fixed-rate swap rate for that currency for the fixed leg, and at LIBOR or the relevant reference rate for the floating leg.

Example 4.1:   Bond issue and associated cross-currency swap

We illustrate currency swaps with an example from the market. A subsidiary of a US bank that invests in projects in the United States issues paper in markets around the world, in response to investor demand worldwide. The company's funding requirement is in US dollars, however it is active in issuing bonds in various currencies, according to where the most favourable conditions can be obtained. When an issue of debt is made in a currency other than dollars, the proceeds must be swapped into dollars for use in the USA, and interest payable on the swapped (dollar) proceeds. To facilitate this the issuer will enter into a currency swap. One of the bank's issues was a Swiss franc step-up bond, part of an overall Euro-MTN programme. The details of the bond are summarised below.

Issue date   March 1998
Maturity   March 2003
Size   CHF 15 million
Coupon   2.40% to 25/3/99
              2.80% to 25/3/00
              3.80% to 25/3/01
              4.80% to 25/3/02

The bond was also callable on each anniversary from March 1999 onwards, and in fact was called by the issuer at the earliest opportunity. The issuing bank entered into a currency swap that resulted in the exchange of principals and the Swiss franc interest payments to be made by the swap counterparty; in return it paid US dollar three-month LIBOR during the life of the swap. At the prevailing spot rate on the effective date, CHF 15 million was exchanged for $10.304 million; these exact same amounts would be exchanged back on the maturity of the swap. When the issue was called the swap was cancelled and the swap counterparty paid a cancellation fee. The interest payment dates on the fixed leg of the swap matched the coupon dates of the bond exactly, as shown above. The floating leg of the swap paid US dollar LIBOR on a quarterly basis, as required by the bond issuer.

The structure is shown in Figure 4.4. A currency swap structure enables a bank or corporate to borrow money in virtually any currency in which a liquid swap market exists, and swap this into a currency that is required. In our example the US bank was able to issue a bond that was attractive to investors. The swap mechanism also hedged the interest rate exposure on the Swiss franc note. The liability remaining for the issuer was quarterly floating-rate interest on US dollars as part of the swap transaction.

4.6   An overview of interest rate swap applications

In this section we review some of the principal uses of swaps as a hedging tool for bond instruments and also how to hedge a swap book.

4.6.1 Corporate applications

Swaps are part of the over-the-counter (OTC) market and so they can be tailored to suit the particular requirements of the user. It is common for swaps to be structured so that they match particular payment dates, payment frequencies and LIBOR margins, which may characterise the underlying exposure of the customer. As the market in interest rate swaps is so large, liquid and competitive, banks are willing to quote rates and structure swaps for virtually all customers, although it

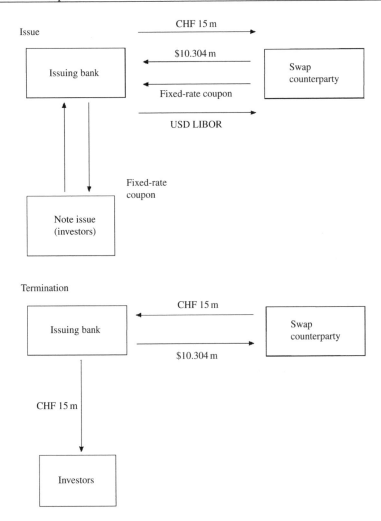

Figure 4.4: Bond issue with currency swap structure

may be difficult for smaller customers to obtain competitive price quotes as notional values below £10 million or £5 million.

Swap applications can be viewed as being one of two main types, asset-linked swaps and liability-linked swaps. Asset-linked swaps are created when the swap is linked to an asset such as a bond in order to change the characteristics of the income stream for investors. Liability-linked swaps are traded when borrowers of funds wish to change the pattern of their cash flows. Of course, just as with repo transactions, the designation of a swap in such terms depends on from whose

Figure 4.5: Changing liability from floating to fixed rate

point of view one is looking at the swap. An asset-linked swap hedge is a liability-linked hedge for the counterparty, except in the case of swap market making banks who make two-way quotes in the instruments.

A straightforward application of an interest rate swap is when a borrower wishes to convert a floating-rate liability into a fixed-rate one, usually in order to remove the exposure to upward moves in interest rates. For instance a company may wish to fix its financing costs. Let us assume a company currently borrowing money at a floating rate, say six-month LIBOR + 100 basis points fears that interest rates may rise in the remaining three years of its loan. It enters into a three-year semi-annual interest rate swap with a bank, as the fixed-rate payer, paying say 6.75% against receiving six-month LIBOR. This fixes the company's borrowing costs for three years at 7.75% (7.99% effective annual rate). This is shown in Figure 4.5.

Example 4.3: Liability-linked swap, fixed- to floating- to fixed-rate exposure

A corporate borrows for five years at a rate of 61/4% and shortly after enters into a swap paying floating rate, so that its net borrowing cost is LIBOR + 40 bps. After one year swap rates have fallen such that the company is quoted four-year swap rates as 4.90–84%. The company decides to switch back into fixed-rate liability in order to take advantage of the lower interest rate environment. It enters into a second swap paying fixed at 4.90% and receiving LIBOR. The net borrowing cost is now 5.30%. The arrangement is illustrated in Figure 4.6. The company has saved 95 basis points on its original borrowing cost, which is the difference between the two swap rates.

Asset-linked swap structures might be required when for example, investors require a fixed interest security when floating-rate assets are available. Borrowers often issue FRNs, the holders of which may prefer to switch the income stream into fixed coupons. As an example, consider a local authority pension fund holding two-year floating-rate gilts. This is an asset of the highest quality, paying LIBID minus 12.5 bps. The pension fund wishes to swap the cash flows to create a fixed-interest asset. It obtains a quote for a tailor-made swap where the floating leg pays LIBID, the quote being 5.55–50%. By entering into this swap the pension fund has in place a structure that pays a fixed coupon of 5.375%. This is shown in Figure 4.7.

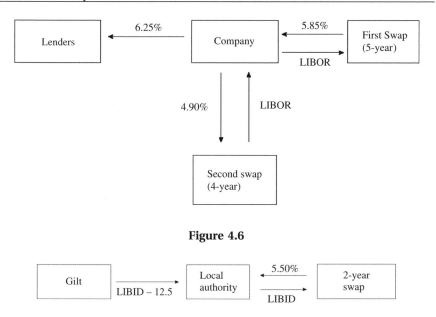

Figure 4.6

Figure 4.7: Transforming a floating-rate asset to fixed rate

4.6.2 Hedging bond instruments using interest rate swaps

We illustrate here a generic approach to the hedging of bond positions using interest rate swaps. The bond trader has the option of using other bonds, bond futures or bond options, as well as swaps, when hedging the interest rate risk exposure of a bond position. However swaps are particularly efficient instruments to use because they display positive convexity characteristics, that is the increase in value of a swap for a fall in interest rates exceeds the loss in value with a similar magnitude rise in rates. This is exactly the price/yield profile of vanilla bonds.

The primary risk measure we require when hedging using a swap is its present value of a basis point or PVBP.[4] This measures the price sensitivity of the swap for a basis point change in interest rates. The PVBP measure is used to calculate the hedge ratio when hedging a bond position. The PVBP can be given by

$$PVBP = \frac{\text{Change in swap value}}{\text{Rate change in base points}} \qquad (4.23)$$

---

[4] This is also known as DVBP or dollar value of a basis point in the US market.

Interest rate swap			
Term to maturity	5 years		
Fixed leg	6.50%		
Basis	Semi-annual, act/365		
Floating leg	6-month LIBOR		
Basis	Semi-annual, act/365		
Nominal amount	£1,000,000		
		Present value (£)	
	Rate change – 10 bps	0 bps	Rate change + 10 bps
Fixed-coupon bond	1,004,940	1,000,000	995,171
Floating-rate bond	1,000,640	1,000,000	999,371
Swap	4,264	0	4,236

Figure 4.8: PVBP for interest rate swap

which can be written as

$$PVBP = \frac{dS}{dr} \qquad (4.24)$$

Using the basic relationship for the value of a swap, which is viewed as the difference between the values of a fixed-coupon bond and an equivalent-maturity floating-rate bond (see Table 4.1) we can also write

$$PVBP = \frac{d\text{Fixed bond}}{dr} - \frac{d\text{Floating bond}}{dr} \qquad (4.25)$$

which essentially states that the basis point value of the swap is the difference in the basis point values of the fixed-coupon and floating-rate bonds. The value is usually calculated for a notional £1 million of swap. The calculation is based on the duration and modified duration calculations used for bonds[5] and assumes that there is a parallel shift in the yield curve.

Figure 4.8 illustrates how equations (4.24) and (4.25) can be used to obtain the PVBP of a swap. Hypothetical five-year bonds are used in the example. The PVBP for a bond can be calculated using Bloomberg or the MDURATION function on Microsoft Excel. Using either of the two equations above we see that the PVBP of the swap is £425.00. This is shown below.

---

[5]   See Chapter 2.

Calculating the PVBP using equation (4.24) we have:

$$PVBP_{swap} = \frac{dS}{dr} = \frac{4264 - (-4236)}{20} = 425 \qquad (4.26)$$

while using equation (4.25) we obtain the same result using the bond values

$$
\begin{aligned}
PVBP_{swap} &= PVBP_{fixed} - PVBP_{floating} \\
&= \frac{1004940 - 995171}{20} - \frac{1000640 - 999371}{20} \\
&= 488.45 - 63.45 \\
&= 425.00
\end{aligned}
\qquad (4.27)
$$

The swap basis point value is lower than that of the five-year fixed-coupon bond, that is £425 compared to £488.45. This is because of the impact of the floating-rate bond risk measure, which reduces the risk exposure of the swap as a whole by £63.45. As a rough rule of thumb, the PVBP of a swap is approximately equal to that of a fixed-rate bond that has a maturity similar to the period from the next coupon reset date of the swap through to the maturity date of the swap. This means that a 10-year semi-annual paying swap would have a PVBP close to that of a 9.5-year fixed-rate bond, and a 5.50-year swap would have a PVBP similar to that of a 5-year bond.

When using swaps as hedge tools, we bear in mind that over time the PVBP of swaps behaves differently to that of bonds. Immediately preceding an interest reset date the PVBP of a swap will be near-identical to that of the same-maturity fixed-rate bond, because the PVBP of a floating-rate bond at this time has essentially nil value. Immediately after the reset date the swap PVBP will be near-identical to that of a bond that matures at the next reset date. This means that at the point (and this point only) right after the reset the swap PVBP will decrease by the amount of the floating-rate PVBP. In between reset dates the swap PVBP is quite stable, as the effects of the fixed- and floating-rate PVBP changes cancel each other out. Contrast this with the fixed-rate PVBP, which decreases in value over time in stable fashion.[6] This feature is illustrated in Figure 4.9. A slight anomaly is that the PVBP of a swap actually increases by a small amount between reset dates; this is because the PVBP of a floating-rate bond decreases at a slightly faster rate than that of the fixed-rate bond during this time.

Hedging bond instruments with interest rate swaps is conceptually similar to hedging with another bond or with bond futures contracts. If one is holding a long position in a vanilla bond, the hedge requires a long position in the swap: remember that a long position in a swap is to be paying fixed (and receiving floating). This hedges the receipt of fixed from the bond position. The change in the value of the swap will match the change in value of the bond, only in the

---

[6]   This assumes no large-scale sudden yield movements.

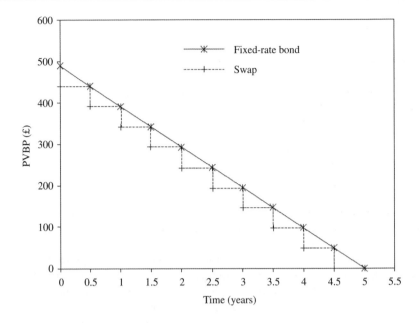

Figure 4.9: PVBP of 5-year swap

opposite direction.[7] The maturity of the swap should match as closely as possible that of the bond. As swaps are OTC contracts, it should be possible to match interest dates as well as maturity dates. If one is short the bond, the hedge is to be short the swap, so the receipt of fixed matches the pay-fixed liability of the short bond position.

The correct nominal amount of the swap to put on is established using the PVBP hedge ratio. This is given as

$$\text{Hedge ratio} = \frac{PVBP_{bond}}{PVBP_{swap}} \qquad (4.28)$$

This technique is still used in the market but suffers from the assumption of parallel yield curve shifts and can therefore lead to significant hedging error at times. More advanced techniques are used by banks when hedging books using swaps, which space does not permit any discussion of. Some of these techniques are discussed in the bibliography.

---

[7]   The change will not be an exact mirror. It is very difficult to establish a precise hedge for a number of reasons, which include differences in day count bases, maturity mismatches and basis risk.

Selected bibliography and references

Bicksler, J., Chen, A., "An Economic Analysis of Interest Rate Swaps", *Journal of Finance* 41(3), 1986, pp. 645–655

Brotherton-Ratcliffe, R., Iben, B., "Yield Curve Applications of Swap Products", in Schwartz, R., Smith, C. (eds), *Advanced Strategies in Financial Risk Management*, New York Institute of Finance 1993

Choudhry, M., *Bond Market Securities*, FT Prentice Hall 2001

Das, S., *Swaps and Financial Derivatives*, 2nd edition, IFR Publishing 1994

Decovny, S., *Swaps*, 2nd edition, FT Prentice Hall 1998

Dunbar, N., "Swaps volumes see euro wane", *Risk*, September 2000

Eales, B., *Financial Risk Management*, McGraw-Hill 1995, Chapter 3

Fabozzi, F. (editor), *Perspectives on Interest Rate Risk Management for Money Managers and Traders*, FJF Associates 1998

Gup, B., Brooks, R., *Interest Rate Risk Management*, Irwin 1993

Henna, P., *Interest-rate Risk Management using Futures and Swaps*, Probus 1991

International Swaps and Derivatives Association, *Code of Standard Working, Assumptions and Provisions for Swaps*, New York, 1991

Jarrow, R., Turnbull, S., *Derivative Securities*, 2nd edition, South-Western 2000

Khan, M., "Online platforms battle for business", *Risk*, September 2000

Kolb, R., *Futures, Options and Swaps*, 3rd edition, Blackwell 2000

Li, A., Raghavan, V. R., "LIBOR-In-Arrears Swaps", *Journal of Derivatives* 3, Spring 1996, pp. 44–48

Lindsay, R., "High Wire Act", *Risk*, August 2000

Marshall, J., Kapner, K., *Understanding Swap Finance*, South-Western 1990

Turnbull, S., "Swaps: A Zero Sum Game", *Financial Management* 16, Spring 1987, pp. 15–21

Glossary

A

Accrued interest: The proportion of interest or coupon earned on an investment from the previous coupon payment date until the value date.

Accrued benefit obligation: Present value of pension benefits that have been earned by an employee to date, whether vested in the employee or not. It can be an important measure when managing the asset/liability ratio of pension funds.

Accumulated value: The same as **Future value**.

ACT/360:   A day/year count convention taking the number of calendar days in a period and a "year" of 360 days.

ACT/365:   A day/year convention taking the number of calendar days in a period and a "year" of 365 days. Under the ISDA definitions used for interest rate swap documentation, ACT/365 means the same as **ACT/ACT**.

ACT/ACT: A day/year count convention taking the number of calendar days in a period and a year equal to the number of days in the current coupon period, multiplied by the coupon frequency. For an interest rate swap, that part of the interest period falling in a leap year is divided by 366 and the remainder is divided by 365.

Add on factor: Simplified estimate of the potential future increase in the replacement cost, or market value, of a derivative transaction.

All-in price: See "dirty price".

Amortising: An amortising principal is one which decreases during the life of a deal, or is repaid in stages during a loan. Amortising an amount over a period of time also means accruing for it pro rata over the period. See **Bullet**.

Annuity: An investment providing a series of (generally equal) future cash flows.

Appreciation: An increase in the market value of a currency in terms of other currencies.

Arbitrage: The process of buying securities in one country, currency or market, and selling identical securities in another to take advantage of price differences. When this is carried out simultaneously, it is in theory a risk-free transaction. There are many forms of arbitrage transactions. For instance in the cash market a bank might issue a money market instrument in one money centre and invest the same amount in another centre at a higher rate, such as an issue of three-month US dollar CDs in the United States at 5.5% and a purchase of three-month

Eurodollar CDs at 5.6%. In the futures market arbitrage might involve buying three-month contracts and selling forward six-month contracts.

Arbitrageur: Someone who undertakes arbitrage trading.

Ask: See **Offer**.

Asset: Probable future economic benefit obtained or controlled as a result of past events or transactions. Generally classified as either current or long-term.

Asset & Liability Management (ALM): The practice of matching the term structure and cash flows of an organisation's asset and liability portfolios to maximise returns and minimise risk.

Asset allocation: Distribution of investment funds within an asset class or across a range of asset classes for the purpose of diversifying risk or adding value to a portfolio.

Asset securitisation: The process whereby loans, receivables and other illiquid assets in the balance sheet are packaged into interest-bearing securities that offer attractive investment opportunities.

Asset-backed security: A security which is collateralised by specific assets, such as mortgages, rather than by the intangible creditworthiness of the issuer.

Asset swap: An interest rate swap or currency swap used in conjunction with an underlying asset such as a bond investment. See **Liability swap**.

At-the-money (ATM): An option is at-the-money if the current value of the underlying is the same as the strike price.

Auction: A method of issue where institutions submit bids to the issuer on a price or yield basis. Auction rules vary considerably across markets.

B

Backwardation: The situation when a forward or futures price for something is lower than the spot price (the same as forward discount in foreign exchange).

Balance sheet: Statement of the financial position of an enterprise at a specific point in time, giving assets, *liabilities* and stockholders' equity.

Banker's acceptance: See **Bill of exchange**.

Base currency: Exchange rates are quoted in terms of the number of units of one currency (the variable or counter currency) which corresponds to one unit of the other currency (the base currency).

Basis: The underlying cash market price minus the futures price. In the case of a bond futures contract, the futures price must be multiplied by the conversion factor for the cash bond in question.

Basis points: In interest rate quotations, 0.01 per cent.

Basis risk: A form of market risk that arises whenever one kind of risk exposure is hedged with an instrument that behaves in a similar, but not necessarily identical way. For instance a bank trading desk may use three-month interest rate futures to hedge its commercial paper or euronote programme. Although eurocurrency rates, to which futures prices respond, are well correlated with commercial paper rates, they do not always move in lock step. If therefore commercial paper rates move by ten basis points but futures prices dropped by only seven basis points, the three basis point gap would be the basis risk.

Basis swap: An interest rate swap where both legs are based on floating rate payments.

Basis trade: Buying the basis means selling a futures contract and buying the commodity or instrument underlying the futures contract. Selling the basis is the opposite.

Bearer bond: A bond for which physical possession of the certificate is proof of ownership. The issuer does not know the identity of the bondholder. Traditionally the bond carries detachable coupon, one for each interest payment date, which are posted to the issuer when payment is due. At maturity the bond is redeemed by sending in the certificate for repayment. These days bearer bonds are usually settled electronically, and while no register of ownership is kept by the issuer, coupon payments may be made electronically.

Bear spread: A spread position taken with the expectation of a fall in value in the underlying.

Benchmark: A bond whose terms set a standard for the market. The benchmark usually has the greatest liquidity, the highest turnover and is usually the most frequently quoted. It also usually trades expensive to the yield curve, due to higher demand for it amongst institutional investors.

Beta: The sensitivity of a stock relative to swings in the overall market. The market has a beta of one, so a stock or portfolio with a beta greater than one will rise or fall more than the overall market, whereas a beta of less than one means that the stock is less volatile.

Bid: The price at which a market maker will buy bonds. A tight bid–offer spread is indicative of a liquid and competitive market. The bid rate in a **Repo** is the interest rate at which the dealer will borrow the **Collateral** and lend the cash. See **Offer**.

Bid figure: In a foreign exchange quotation, the exchange rate omitting the last two decimal places. For example, when EUR/USD is 1.1910/20, the big figure is 1.19. See **Points**.

Bid–Offer: The two-way price at which a market will buy and sell stock.

Bill: A bill of exchange is a payment order written by one person (the drawer) to another, directing the latter (drawee) to pay a certain amount of money at a future date to a third party. A bill of exchange is a bank draft when drawn on a bank. By accepting the draft, a bank agrees to pay the face value of the obligation if the drawer fails to pay, hence the term banker's acceptance. A Treasury bill is short-term government paper of up to one year's maturity, sold at a discount to principal value and redeemed at par.

Bill of exchange: A short-term, **Zero-coupon** debt issued by a company to finance commercial trading. If it is guaranteed by a bank, it becomes a banker's acceptance.

Black-Scholes: A widely used option pricing formula devised by Fischer Black and Myron Scholes.

Bloomberg: The trading, analytics and news service produced by Bloomberg L.P., also used to refer to the terminal itself.

Bond basis: An interest rate is quoted on a bond basis if it is on an **ACT/365**, **ACT/ACT** or 30/360 basis. In the short term (for accrued interest, for example), these three are different. Over a whole (non-leap) year, however they all equate to 1. In general, the expression "bond basis" does not distinguish between them and is calculated as ACT/365. See **Money-market basis**.

Bond-equivalent yield: The yield which would be quoted on a US treasury bond which is trading at par and which has the same economic return and maturity as a given treasury bill.

Bootstrapping: Building up successive zero-coupon yields from a combination of coupon-bearing yields.

Bpv: Basis point value. The price movement due to a one basis point change in yield.

Broker-dealers: Members of the London Stock Exchange who may intermediate between customers and market makers; may also act as principals, transacting business with customers from their own holdings of stock.

Bulldog: Sterling domestic bonds issued by non-UK domiciled borrowers. These bonds trade under a similar arrangement to gilts and are settled via the Central Gilts Office (now CREST).

Bullet: A loan/deposit has a bullet maturity if the principal is all repaid at maturity. See **Amortising**.

Buy/sell-back: Opposite of **Sell/buy-back**.

C

Cable: The exchange rate for sterling against the US dollar.

CAD: The European Union's Capital Adequacy Directive.

Callable bond: A bond which provides the borrower with an option to redeem the issue before the original maturity date. In most cases certain terms are set before the issue, such as the date after which the bond is callable and the price at which the issuer may redeem the bond.

Call option: An option to purchase the commodity or instrument underlying the option. See **Put**.

Call price: The price at which the issuer can call in a bond or preferred bond.

Capital market: Long-term market (generally longer than one year) for financial instruments. See **Money market**.

CBOT: The Chicago Board of Trade, one of the two futures exchanges in Chicago, USA and one of the largest in the world.

CD: See **Certificate of deposit**.

Central Gilts Office: The office of the Bank of England which runs the computer-based settlement system for gilt-edged securities and certain other securities (mostly bulldogs) for which the Bank acts as Registrar.

Certificate of Deposit (CD):   A money market instrument of up to one year's maturity (although CDs of up to five years have been issued) that pays a bullet interest payment on maturity. After issue, CDs can trade freely in the secondary market, the ease of which is a function of the credit quality of the issuer.

CGBR: Central Government Borrowing Requirement.

CGNCR: Central Government Net Cash Requirement.

CGO reference prices: Daily prices of gilt-edged and other securities held in CGO which are used by CGO in various processes, including revaluing stock loan transactions, calculating total consideration in a repo transaction, and **DBV** assembly.

Cheapest to deliver: (Or **CTD**). In a bond futures contract, the one underlying bond among all those that are deliverable, which is the most price-efficient for the seller to deliver.

Classic repo: Repo is short for "sale and repurchase agreement" – a simultaneous spot sale and forward purchase of a security, equivalent to borrowing money against a loan of collateral. A reverse repo is the opposite. The terminology is usually applied from the perspective of the repo dealer. For example, when a central bank does repos, it is lending cash (the repo dealer is borrowing cash from the central bank).

Clean deposit: The same as **Time deposit**.

Clean price: The price of a bond excluding accrued coupon. The price quoted in the market for a bond is generally a clean price rather than a **Dirty price**.

Close-out netting: The ability to net a portfolio of contracts with a given counterparty in the event of default.

CMO: Central Moneymarkets Office which settles transactions in Treasury bills and other money market instruments, and provides a depository.

CMTM: Current **mark-to-market** value.

Collateral: Something of value, often of good creditworthiness such as a government bond, given temporarily to a counterparty to enhance a party's creditworthiness. In a **repo**, the collateral is actually sold temporarily by one party to the other rather than merely lodged with it.

Commercial paper: A short-term security issued by a company or bank, generally with a zero coupon.

Competitive bid: A bid for the stock at a price stated by a bidder in an auction. Non-competitive bid is a bid where no price is specified; such bids are allotted at the weighted average price of successful competitive bid prices.

Compound interest: When some interest on an investment is paid before maturity and the investor can reinvest it to earn interest on interest, the interest is said to be compounded. Compounding generally assumes that the reinvestment rate is the same as the original rate. See **Simple interest**.

Consideration: The total price paid in a transaction, including taxes, commissions and (for bonds) accrued interest.

Continuous compounding: A mathematical, rather than practical, concept of compound interest where the period of compounding is infinitesimally small.

Contract date: The date on which a transaction is negotiated. See **Value date**.

Contract for differences:

Conventional gilts (including double-dated): Gilts on which interest payments and principal repayments are fixed.

Conversion factor: In a bond futures contract, a factor to make each deliverable bond comparable with the contract's notional bond specification. Define as the price of one unit of the deliverable bond required to make its yield equal to the notional coupon. The price paid for a bond on delivery is the futures settlement price times the conversion factor.

Convertible currency: A currency that may be freely exchanged for other currencies.

Convexity: A measure of the curvature of a bond's price/yield curve

$$\left(\text{mathematically, } \frac{d^2 P}{dr^2} \text{ dirty price} \right)$$

Cost of carry: The net running cost of holding a position (which may be negative), for example, the cost of borrowing cash to buy a bond less the coupon earned on the bond while holding it.

Coupon: The interest payment(s) made by the issuer of security to the holders, based on the coupon rate and the face value.

Cover: To cover an exposure is to deal in such a way as to remove the risk – either reversing the position, or hedging it by dealing in an instrument with a similar but opposite risk profile. Also the amount by how much a bond auction is subscribed.

CP: See **Commercial paper**.

Credit (or default) risk: The risk that a loss will be incurred if a counterparty to a derivatives transaction does not fulfil its financial obligations in a timely manner.

Credit derivatives: Financial contracts that involve a potential exchange of payments in which at least one of the cash flows is linked to the performance of a specified underlying credit-sensitive asset or liability.

Credit spread: The interest rate spread between two debt issues of similar duration and maturity, reflecting the relative creditworthiness of the issuers.

Credit default swap: A bilateral OTC contract between two parties who have exchanged credit risk from one party to the other in return for a specified premium. The credit risk is that pertaining to a specified reference asset or reference entity, and on occurrence of a pre-defined credit event the party to whom the credit risk of the reference asset has been transferred will pay the nominal value of the credit default swap contract to the party that has transferred the credit risk. The former party is known as the protection seller and the latter party is known as the protection buyer. On occurrence of the credit event, the contract terminates and the protection seller makes the payment to the protection buyer.

Credit swaps: Agreement between two counterparties to exchange disparate cash flows, at least one of which must be tied to the performance of a credit-sensitive asset or to a portfolio or index of such assets. The other cash flow is usually tied to a **Floating rate** index (such as **LIBOR**) or a fixed rate or is linked to another credit-sensitive asset.

CREST: The paperless share settlement system through which trades conducted on the London Stock Exchange can be settled. The system is operated by CRESTCo and was introduced in 1996.

CRND: Commissioners for the Reduction of the National Debt, formally responsible for investment of funds held within the public sector, e.g. National Insurance Fund.

Cross: See **Cross-rate**.

Cross-rate: Generally an exchange rate between two currencies, neither of which is the US dollar. In the American market, spot cross is the exchange rate for US dollars against Canadian dollars in its direct form.

CTD: See **Cheapest to deliver**.

Cum dividend: Literally "with dividend", stock that is traded with interest or dividend accrued included in the price.

Current yield: Bond coupon as a proportion of clean price per 100; does not take principal gain/loss or time value of money into account. See **Yield to maturity**, **Simple yield to maturity**.

D

Day count: The convention used to calculate accrued interest on bonds and interest on cash. For UK gilts the convention changed to **actual/actual** from **actual/365** on 1 November 1998. For cash the convention in sterling markets is **actual/365**.

DBV (delivery by value):   A mechanism whereby a CGO member may borrow from or lend money to another CGO member against overnight gilt collateral. The CGO system automatically selects and delivers securities to a specified aggregate value on the basis of the previous night's CGO reference prices; equivalent securities are returned the following day. The DBV functionality allows the giver and taker of collateral to specify the classes of security to include within the DBV. The options are: all classes of security held within CGO, including strips and bulldogs; coupon bearing gilts and bulldogs; coupon bearing gilts and strips; only coupon bearing gilts.

Debenture: In the US market, an unsecured domestic bond, backed by the general credit quality of the issuer. Debentures are issued under a trust deed or indenture. In the UK market, a bond that is secured against the general assets of the issuer.

Debt Management Office (DMO):   An executive arm of the UK Treasury, responsible for cash management of the government's borrowing requirement. This includes responsibility for issuing government bonds (gilts), a function previously carried out by the Bank of England. The DMO began operations in April 1998.

Deliverable bond: One of the bonds which is eligible to be delivered by the seller of a bond futures contract at the contract's maturity, according to the specifications of that particular contract.

Delivery: Transfer of gilts (in settlements) from seller to buyer.

Delivery versus payment (DVP):   The simultaneous exchange of securities and cash. The assured payment mechanism of the CGO achieves the same protection.

Derivative: Strictly, any financial instrument whose value is derived from another, such as a forward foreign exchange rate, a futures contract, an option, an interest rate swap, etc. Forward deals to be settled in full are not always called derivatives, however.

Devaluation: An official one-off decrease in the value of a currency in terms of other currencies.

Dirty price: The price of a bond including accrued interest. Also known as the "all-in" price.

Discount: The amount by which a currency is cheaper, in terms of another currency, for future delivery than for spot, is the forward discount (in general, a reflection of interest rate differentials between two currencies). If an exchange rate is "at a discount" (without specifying to which of the two currencies this refers), this generally means that the **Variable currency** is at a discount. See **Premium**.

Discount house: In the UK money market, originally securities houses that dealt directly with the Bank of England in T-bills and bank bills, or discount instruments, hence the name. Most discount houses were taken over by banking groups and the term is not generally used, as the BoE now also deals directly with clearing banks and securities houses.

Discount rate: The method of market quotation for certain securities (US and UK treasury bills, for example), expressing the return on the security as a proportion of the face value of the security received at maturity – as opposed to a **Yield** which expresses the yield as a proportion of the original investment.

DMO: The UK Debt Management Office.

DMR: The Debt Management Report, published annually by HM Treasury.

DRM: Debt and Reserves Management Team in HM Treasury.

Duration: A measure of the weighted average life of a bond or other series of cash flows, using the present values of the cash flows as the weights. See **Modified duration**.

Duration gap: Measurement of the interest rate exposure of an institution.

Duration weighting: The process of using the modified duration value for bonds to calculate the exact nominal holdings in a spread position. This is necessary because £1 million nominal of a two-year bond is not equivalent to £1 million of say, a five-year bond. The modified duration value of the five-year bond will be higher, indicating that its "basis point value" (bpv) will be greater, and that therefore £1 million worth of this bond represents greater sensitivity to a move in interest rates (risk). As another example consider a fund manager holding £10 million of five-year bonds. The fund manager wishes to switch into a holding of two-year bonds with the same overall risk position. The basis point values of the bonds are 0.041583 and 0.022898 respectively. The ratio of the bpvs is 0.041583/ 0.022898 = 1.816. The fund manager therefore needs to switch into £10m × 1.816 = £18.160 million of the two-year bond.

DVP: Delivery versus payment, in which the settlement mechanics of a sale or loan of securities against cash is such that the securities and cash are exchanged against each other simultaneously through the same clearing mechanism and neither can be transferred unless the other is.

E

Early exercise: The exercise or assignment of an option prior to expiration.

ECU: The European Currency Unit, a basket composed of European Union currencies, now defunct following the introduction of euro currency.

Effective rate: An effective interest rate is the rate which, earned as simple interest over one year, gives the same return as interest paid more frequently than once per year and then compounded. See **Nominal rate**.

Embedded option: Interest rate-sensitive option in debt instrument that affects its redemption. Such instruments include **Mortgage-backed securities** and **Callable bonds**.

Equity: The residual interest in the net assets of an entity that remains after deducting the liabilities.

Equity options: Options on shares of an individual common stock.

Equity warrant: Warranty, usually attached to a bond, entitling the holder to purchase share(s).

Euribor: The reference rate for the euro currency, set in Frankfurt.

Euro: The name for the domestic currency of the European Monetary Union. Not to be confused with **Eurocurrency**.

Euroclear: An international clearing system for Eurocurrency and international securities. Euroclear is based in Brussels and managed by Morgan Guaranty Trust Company.

Eurocurrency: A Eurocurrency is a currency owned by a non-resident of the country in which the currency is legal tender. Not to be confused with **Euro.**

Euro-issuance: The issue of gilts (or other securities) denominated in euros.

Euromarket: The international market in which **Eurocurrencies** traded.

European: A European **Option** is one that may be exercised only at **Expiry**.

Exchange controls: Regulations restricting the free convertibility of a currency into other currencies.

Exchange rate agreement: A contract for differences based on the movement in a forward–forward foreign exchange swap price. Does not take account of the effect of **Spot** rate changes as an FXA does. See **SAFE**.

Exchange-traded: **Futures** contracts are traded on a futures exchange, as opposed to forward deals which are **OTC**. **Option** contracts are similarly exchange traded rather than **OTC**.

Ex-dividend (xd) date: A bond's record date for the payment of coupons. The coupon payment will be made to the person who is the registered holder of the stock on the xd date. For UK gilts this is seven working days before the coupon date.

Exercise: To exercise an **Option** (by the holder) is to require the other party (the **Writer**) to fulfil the underlying transaction. Exercise price is the same as **Strike** price.

Expected (credit) loss: Estimate of the amount a derivatives counterparty is likely to lose as a result of default from a derivatives contract, with a given level of probability. The expected loss of any derivative position can be derived by combining the distributions of credit exposures, rate of recovery and probabilities of default.

Expected rate of recovery: See **Rate of recovery**.

Expiry: An option's expiry is the time after which it can no longer be **Exercised**.

Exposure: Risk to market movements.

Exposure profile: The path of worst-case or expected exposures over time. Different instruments reveal quite differently-shaped exposures profiles due to the interaction of the diffusion and amortisation effects.

Extrapolation: The process of estimating a price or rate for a particular value date, from other "known" prices, when the value date required lies outside the period covered by the known prices.

F

Face value: The principal amount of a security generally repaid ("redeemed") all at maturity, but sometimes repaid in stages, on which the **Coupon** amounts are calculated.

Fixing: See **Libor fixing**.

Floating rate: An interest rate set with reference to an external index. Also an instrument paying a floating rate is one where the rate of interest is refixed in line with market conditions at regular intervals such as every three or six months. In the current market, an exchange rate determined by market forces with no government intervention.

Floating rate CD: CD on which the rate of interest payable is refixed in line with market conditions at regular intervals (usually six months).

Floating rate gilt: Gilt issued with an interest rate adjusted periodically in line with market interbank rates.

Floating rate note: **Capital market** instrument on which the rate of interest payable is refixed in line with market conditions at regular intervals (usually six months).

Forward rate agreement (FRA):   Short-term interest rate hedge. Specifically, a contract between buyer and seller for an agreed interest rate on a notional deposit of a specified maturity on a predetermined future date. No principal is exchanged. At maturity the seller pays the buyer the difference if rates have risen above the agreed level, and vice versa.

FRN: See **Floating rate note**.

FSA: The Financial Services Authority, the body responsible for the regulation of investment business, and the supervision of banks and money market institutions in the UK. The FSA took over these duties from nine "self-regulatory organisations" that had previously carried out this function, including the Securities and Futures Authority (SFA), which had been responsible for regulation of professional investment business in the City of London. The FSA commenced its duties in 1998.

FTSE-100:   Index comprising 100 major UK shares listed on The International Stock Exchange in London. Futures and options on the index are traded at the London International Financial Futures and Options Exchange (**LIFFE**).

Fungible: A financial instrument that is equivalent in value to another, and easily exchanged or substituted. The best example is cash money, as a £10 note has the same value and is directly exchangeable with another £10 note. A bearer bond also has this quality.

Future: A futures contract is a contract to buy or sell securities or other goods at a future date at a predetermined price. Futures contracts are usually standardised and traded on an exchange.

Future exposure: See **Potential exposure**.

Future value: The amount of money achieved in the future, including interest, by investing a given amount of money now. See **Time value of money**, **Present value**.

Futures contract: A deal to buy or sell some financial instrument or commodity for value on a future date. Unlike a forward deal, futures contracts are traded only on an exchange (rather than **OTC**), have standardised contract sizes and value dates, and are often only **Contract for differences** rather than deliverable.

G

G7:   The "Group of Seven" countries, the USA, Canada, UK, Germany, France, Italy and Japan.

GDP: Gross domestic product, the value of total output produced within a country's borders.

GEMM: A gilt-edged market maker, a bank or securities house registered with the Bank of England as a market maker in gilts. A GEMM is required to meet certain obligations as part of its function as a registered market maker, including making two-way price quotes at all times in all gilts and taking part in gilt auctions. The

Debt Management Office now make a distinction between conventional gilt GEMMs and index-linked GEMMs, known as IG GEMMs.

General collateral (GC):   Securities, which are not "special", used as collateral against cash borrowing. A repo buyer will accept GC at any time that a specific stock is not quoted as required in the transaction. In the gilts market GC includes **DBVs**.

GIC: Guaranteed investment contract.

Gilt: A UK Government sterling denominated, listed security issued by HM Treasury with initial maturity of over 365 days when issued. The term "gilt" (or gilt-edged) is a reference to the primary characteristic of gilts as an investment: their security.

Gilt-edged market maker: See **GEMM**.

GNP: Gross national product, the total monetary value of a country's output, as produced by citizens of that country.

Gross redemption yield: The same as **Yield to maturity**; "gross" because it does not take tax effects into account.

GRY: See **Gross redemption yield**.

H

Hedge ratio: The ratio of the size of the position it is necessary to take in a particular instrument as a hedge against another, to the size of the position being hedged.

Hedging: Protecting against the risks arising from potential market movements in exchange rates, interest rates or other variables. See **Cover**, **Arbitrage**, **Speculation**.

I

IDB: Inter-Dealer Broker; in this context a broker that provides facilities for dealing in bonds between market makers.

IG: Index-linked gilt whose coupons and final redemption payment are related to the movements in the Retail Price Index (RPI).

Immunisation: This is the process by which a bond portfolio is created that has an assured return for a specific time horizon irrespective of changes in interest rates. The mechanism underlying immunisation is a portfolio structure that balances the change in the value of a portfolio at the end of the investment horizon (time period) with the return gained from the reinvestment of cash flows from the portfolio. As such, immunisation requires the portfolio manager to offset interest-rate risk and reinvestment risk.

Implied repo rate: The break-even interest rate at which it is possible to sell a bond **Futures contract**, buy a **Deliverable bond**, and **Repo** the bond out. See **Cash-and-carry**.

Implied volatility: The **Volatility** used by a dealer to calculate an **Option** price; conversely, the volatility implied by the price actually quoted.

Interbank: The market in unsecured lending and trading between banks of roughly similar credit quality.

Interest rate swap: An agreement to exchange a series of cash flows determined in one currency, based on fixed or **Floating** interest payments on an agreed **Notional** principal, for a series of cash flows based in the same currency but on a different interest rate. May be combined with a **Currency swap**.

Intermarket spread: A spread involving futures contracts in one market spread against futures contracts in another market.

Internal rate of return: The yield necessary to discount a series of cash flows to an **NPV** of zero.

ISMA: The International Securities Market Association. This association drew up with the PSA (now renamed the Bond Market Association) the PSA/ISMA Global Master Repurchase Agreement.

Issuer risk: Risk to an institution when it holds debt securities issued by another institution.

Iteration: The repetitive mathematical process of estimating the answer to a problem, by trying how well this estimate fits the data, adjusting the estimate appropriately and trying against, until the fit is acceptably close. Used, for example, in calculating a bond's **Yield** from its price.

J

Junk bonds: The common term for high-yield bonds; higher risk, low rated debt.

K

Kappa (k):   An alternative term to refer to volatility; see **Vega**.

Knock out/in: A knock out (in) **Option** ceases to exist (starts to exist) if the underlying reaches a certain trigger level.

L

Leverage: The ability to control large amounts of an underlying variable for a small initial investment.

Liability: Probable future sacrifice of economic benefit due to present obligations to transfer assets or provide services to other entities as a result of past events or transactions. Generally classed as either current or long-term.

LIBID: The London Interbank Bid Rate, the rate at which banks will pay for funds in the interbank market.

LIBOR: The London Interbank Offered Rate, the lending rate for all major currencies up to one year set at 11am each day by the British Bankers Association.

Libor fixing: The Libor rate "fixed" by the British Bankers Association (BBA) at 1100 hours each day, for maturities up to one year.

LIFFE: The London International Financial Futures and Options Exchange, the largest futures exchange in Europe.

Limean: The arithmetic average of Libor and Libid rates.

Limit up/down: **Futures** prices are generally not allowed to change by more than a specified total amount in a specified time, in order to control risk in very volatile conditions. The maximum movements permitted are referred to as limit up and limit down.

Liquidation: Any transaction that closes out or offsets a futures or options position.

Liquidity: A word describing the ease with which one can undertake transactions in a particular market or instrument. A market where there are always ready buyers and sellers willing to transact at competitive prices is regarded as liquid. In banking, the term is also used to describe the requirement that a portion of a bank's assets be held in short-term risk free instruments, such as government bonds, T-Bills and high quality **Certificates of Deposit**.

Loan-equivalent amount: Description of derivative exposure which is used to compare the credit risk of derivatives with that of traditional bonds or bank loans.

Lognormal: A variable's **Probability distribution** is lognormal if the logarithm of the variable has a normal distribution.

Lognormal distribution: The assumption that the log of today's interest rate, for example, minus the log of yesterday's rate is normally distributed.

Long: A long position is a surplus of purchases over sales of a given currency or asset, or a situation which naturally gives rise to an organisation benefiting from a strengthening of that currency or asset. To a money market dealer, however, a long position is a surplus of borrowings taken in over money lent out (which gives rise to a benefit if that currency weakens rather than strengthens). See **Short**.

LSE: London Stock Exchange.

M

Macaulay duration: See **Duration**.

Mapping: The process whereby a treasury's derivative positions are related to a set of risk "buckets".

Margin: Initial margin is **Collateral**, placed by one party with a counterparty at the time of the deal, against the possibility that the market price will move against the first party, thereby leaving the counterparty with a credit risk. Variation margin is a payment or extra collateral transferred subsequently from one party to the other because the market price has moved. Variation margin payment is either in effect a settlement of profit/loss (for example, in the case of a **Futures** contract) or the reduction of credit exposure (for example, in the case of a **Repo)**. In gilt **Repos**, variation margin refers to the fluctuation band or threshold within which the existing collateral's value may vary before further cash or **Collateral** needs to be transferred. In a loan, margin is the extra interest above a **Benchmark** (e.g. a margin of 0.5 per cent over LIBOR) required by a lender to compensate for the credit risk of that particular borrower.

Margin call: A request following marking-to-market of a repo transaction for the initial margin to be reinstated or, where no initial margin has been taken to restore the cash/securities ratio to parity.

Margin default rate: See **Probability of default**.

Margin transfer: The payment of a **Margin call**.

Market comparables: Technique for estimating the fair value of an instrument for which no price is quoted by comparing it with the quoted prices of similar instruments.

Market-maker: Market participant who is committed, explicitly or otherwise, to quoting two-way bid and offer prices at all times in a particular market.

Market risk: Risks related to changes in prices of tradeable macroeconomic variables, such as exchange rate risks.

Mark-to-market: The act of revaluing securities to current market values. Such revaluations should include both coupon accrued on the securities outstanding and interest accrued on the cash.

Matched book: This refers to the matching by a repo trader of securities repoed in and out. It carries no implications that the trader's position is "matched" in terms of exposure, for example to short-term interest rates.

Maturity date: Date on which stock is redeemed.

Mean: Average.

Modified following: The convention that if a value date in the future falls on a non-business day, the value date will be moved to the next following business day, unless this moves the value date to the next month, in which case the value date is moved back to the last previous business day.

Money market: Short-term market (generally up to one year) for financial instruments. See **Capital market**.

Money-market basis: An interest rate quoted on an **ACT/360** basis is said to be on a money-market basis. See **Bond basis**.

Monte Carlo simulation: Technique used to determine the likely value of a derivative or other contract by simulating the evolution of the underlying variables many times. The discounted average outcome of the simulation gives an approximation of the derivative's value. Monte Carlo simulation can be used to estimate the **Value-at-risk (VAR)** of a portfolio. Here, it generates a simulation of many correlated market movements for the markets to which the portfolio is exposed, and the positions in the portfolio are revalued repeatedly in accordance with the simulated scenarios. This gives a probability distribution of portfolio gains and losses from which the **VAR** can be determined.

Moosmuller: A method for calculating the yield of a bond.

Mortgage-backed security (MBS): Security guaranteed by pool of mortgages. MBS markets include the US, UK, Japan and Denmark.

Moving average convergence/divergence: The crossing of two exponentially smoothed moving averages that oscillate above and below an equilibrium line. (MACD).

N

Naked: A naked **Option** position is one not protected by an off-setting position in the **Underlying**. See **Covered call/put**.

NAO: National Audit Office.

Negative divergence: When at least two indicators, indexes or averages show conflicting or contradictory trends.

Negotiable: A security which can be bought and sold in a **Secondary market** is negotiable.

Net present value: The net present value of a series of cash flows is the sum of the present values of each cash flow (some or all of which may be negative).

NLF: National Loans Fund, the account which brings together all UK Government lending and borrowing.

Noise: Fluctuations in the market which can confuse or impede interpretation of market direction.

Nominal amount: Same as **Face value** of a security.

Nominal rate: A rate of interest as quoted, rather than the **Effective rate** to which it is equivalent.

Normal: A normal **Probability distribution** is a particular distribution assumed to prevail in a wide variety of circumstances, including the financial markets. Mathematically, it corresponds to the probability density function:

$$\frac{1}{\sqrt{2\pi}} e^{-\frac{1}{2}\sigma^2}$$

Notional: In a bond futures contract, the bond bought or sold is a standardised non-existent notional bond, as opposed to the actual bonds which are **Deliverable** at maturity. **Contracts for differences** also require a notional principal amount on which settlement can be calculated.

Novation: Replacement of a contract or, more usually, a series of contracts with one new contract.

NPV: See **Net present value**.

O

O/N: See **Overnight**.

Odd date: See **Broken date**.

Offer: The price at which a market maker will sell bonds. Also called "ask".

Off-market: A rate which is not the current market rate.

Opening leg: The first half of a repo transaction.

Open interest: The quantity of **Futures** contracts (of a particular specification) which have not yet been closed out by reversing. Either all **Long** positions or all **Short** positions are counted but not both.

Operational Market Notice: Sets out the DMO's (previously the Bank's) operations and procedures in the gilt market.

Operational risk: Risk of loss occurring due to inadequate systems and control, human error, or management failure.

Opportunity cost: Value of an action that could have been taken if the current action had not been chosen.

Option: The right (but not the obligation) to buy or sell securities at a fixed price within a specified period.

Option forward: See **Time option**.

OTC: Over the counter. Strictly speaking any transaction not conducted on a registered stock exchange. Trades conducted via the telephone between banks, and contracts such as FRAs and (non-exchange traded) options are said to be "over-the-counter" instruments. OTC also refers to non-standard instruments or contracts traded between two parties; for example a client with a requirement for a specific risk to be hedged with a tailor-made instrument may enter into an OTC structured option trade with a bank that makes markets in such products.

Over the counter: An OTC transaction is one dealt privately between any two parties, with all details agreed between them, as opposed to one dealt on an exchange – for example, a **Forward** deal as opposed to a **Futures contract**.

Overborrowed: A position in which a dealer's liabilities (borrowings taken in) are of longer maturity than the assets (loans out).

Overlent: A position in which a dealer's assets (loans out) are of longer maturity than the liabilities (borrowings taken in).

Overnight: A deal from today until the next working day ("tomorrow").

P

Paper: Another term for a bond or debt issue.

Par: In foreign exchange, when the outright and **Spot** exchange rates are equal, the **Forward swap** is zero or par. When the price of a security is equal to the face value, usually expressed as 100, it is said to be trading at par. A par swap rate is the current market rate for a fixed **Interest rate swap** against **LIBOR**.

Par yield curve: A curve plotting maturity against **Yield** for bonds priced at par.

Parity: The official rate of exchange for one currency in terms of another which a government is obliged to maintain by means of intervention.

Pips: See **Points**.

Plain vanilla: See **Vanilla.**

Points: The last two decimal places in an exchange rate. For example, when EUR/USD is 1.1910/1.1920, the points are 10/20. See **Bid figure**.

Preference shares: These are a form of corporate financing. They are normally fixed interest shares whose holders have the right to receive dividends ahead of ordinary shareholders. If a company were to go into liquidation, preference shareholders would rank above ordinary shareholders for the repayment of their investment in the company. Preference shares are normally traded within the fixed interest division of a bank or securities house.

Premium: The forward premium is the amount by which a currency is more expensive, in terms of another currency, for future delivery than for spot (in general, a reflection of interest rate differentials between two currencies). If an exchange rate is "at a premium" (without specifying to which of the two currencies this refers), this generally means that the **Variable currency** is at a premium. See **Discount**.

Present value: The amount of money which needs to be invested now to achieve a given amount in the future when interest is added. See **Time value of money, Future value**.

Pre-settlement risk: As distinct from credit risk arising from intra-day settlement risk, this term describes the risk of loss that might be suffered during the life of the contract if a counterparty to a trade defaulted and if, at the time of the default, the instrument had a positive economic value.

Price-earnings ratio: A ratio giving the price of a stock relative to the earnings per share.

Price factor: See **Conversion factor**.

Primary market: The market for new debt, into which new bonds are issued. The primary market is made up of borrowers, investors and the investment banks which place new debt into the market, usually with their clients. Bonds that trade after they have been issued are said to be part of the secondary market.

Probability distribution: The mathematical description of how probable it is that the value of something is less than or equal to a particular level.

Put: A put option is an option to sell the commodity or instrument **Underlying** the option. See **Call**.

Q

Quanto: An option that has its final payoff linked to two or more underlying assets or reference rates.

Quanto swap: A **Swap** where the payments of one or both legs are based on a measurement (such as the interest rate) in one currency but payable in another currency.

Quasi-coupon date: The regular date for which a **Coupon** payment would be scheduled if there were one. Used for price/yield calculations for **Zero-coupon** instruments.

R

Record date: A **Coupon** or other payment due on a security is paid by the issuer to whoever is registered on the record date as being the owner. See **Ex-dividend, Cum dividend**.

Redeem: A security is said to be redeemed when the principal is repaid.

Redemption yield: The rate of interest at which all future payments (coupons and redemption) on "a" bond are discounted so that their total equals the current price of the bond (inversely related to price).

Redenomination: A change in the currency unit in which the nominal value of a security is expressed (in context, from sterling to euro).

Refer: The practice whereby a trader instructs a broker to put "under reference" any prices or rates he has quoted to him, meaning that they are no longer "firm" and the broker must refer to the trader before he can trade on the price initially quoted.

Register: Record of ownership of securities. For gilts, excluding bearer bonds, entry in an official register confers title.

Registered bond: A bond for which the issuer keeps a record (register) of its owners. Transfer of ownership must be notified and recorded in the register. Interest payments are posted (more usually electronically transferred) to the bondholder.

Registrar's department: Department of the Bank of England which maintains the register of holdings of gilts.

Reinvestment rate: The rate at which interest paid during the life of an investment is reinvested to earn interest-on-interest, which in practice will generally not be the same as the original yield quoted on the investment.

Repo: Usually refers in particular to **Classic repo**. Also used as a term to include **Buy/sell-backs** and **Securities lending.**

Repo rate: The return earned on a repo transaction expressed as an interest rate on the cash side of the transaction.

Repurchase agreement: See **Repo**.

Return on assets: The net earnings of a company divided by its assets.

Return on equity: The net earnings of a company divided by its equity.

Reverse: See **Reverse repo**.

Reverse repo: The opposite of a **Repo**.

Rollover: See **Tom/next**. Also refers to a renewal of a loan.

Rump: A gilt issue so designated because it is illiquid, generally because there is a very small nominal amount left in existence.

Running yield: Same as **Current yield**.

S

S/N: See **Spot/next**.

SAFE: See **Synthetic** agreement for forward exchange.

Secondary market: The market in instruments after they have been issued. Bonds are bought and sold after their initial issue by the borrower, and the marketplace for this buying and selling is referred to as the secondary market. The new issues market is the primary market.

Securities and Exchange Commission (SEC):   The central regulatory authority in the United States, responsible for policing the financial markets including the bond markets.

Securities lending: When a specific security is lent against some form of collateral. Also known as stock lending.

Security: A financial asset sold initially for cash by a borrowing organisation (the "issuer"). The security is often negotiable and usually has a maturity date when it is redeemed.

Sell/buy-back: Simultaneous spot sale and forward purchase of a security, with the forward price calculated to achieve an effect equivalent to a **Classic repo.**

Settlement: The process of transferring stock from seller to buyer and arranging the corresponding movement of funds between the two parties.

Settlement bank: Bank which agrees to receive and make assured payments for gilts bought and sold by a CGO member.

Settlement date: Date on which transfers of gilts and payment occur, usually the next working date after the trade is conducted.

Settlement risk: The risk that occurs when there is a non-simultaneous exchange of value. Also known as "delivery risk" and "Herstatt risk".

Short: A short position is a surplus of sales over purchases of a given currency or asset, or a situation which naturally gives rise to an organisation benefiting from a weakening of that currency or asset. To a money market dealer, however, a short position is a surplus of money lent out over borrowings taken in (which give rise to a benefit if that currency strengthens rather than weakens). See **Long.**

Short date: A deal for value on a date other than spot but less than one month after spot.

Simple interest: When interest on an investment is paid all at maturity or not reinvested to earn interest on interest, the interest is said to be simple. See **Compound interest.**

Simple yield to maturity: Bond coupon plus principal gain/loss amortised over the time to maturity, as a proportion of the clean price per 100. Does not take **Time value of money** into account. See **Yield to maturity, Current yield.**

SLA: Service Level Agreement, in this context between the DMO and service suppliers in the Bank and HM Treasury.

Special: A security which for any reason is sought after in the repo market, thereby enabling any holder of the security to earn incremental income (in excess of the General Collateral rate) through lending them via a repo transaction. The repo rate for a special will be below the GC rate, as this is the rate the borrower of the cash is paying in return for supplying the special bond as collateral. An individual security can be in high demand for a variety of reasons, for instance if there is sudden heavy investor demand for it, or (if it is a benchmark issue) it is required as a hedge against a new issue of similar maturity paper.

Speculation: A deal undertaken because the dealer expects prices to move in their favour, as opposed to **Hedging** or **Arbitrage**.

Spot: A deal to be settled on the customary value date for that particular market. In the foreign exchange market, this is for value in two working days' time.

Spot/next: A transaction from **Spot** until the next working day.

Spread: The difference between the bid and offer prices in a quotation. Also a strategy involving the purchase of an instrument and the simultaneous sale of a similar related instrument, such as the purchase of a **Call option** at one **Strike** and the sale of a call option at a different strike.

Square: A position in which sales exactly match purchases, or in which assets exactly match liabilities. See **Long**, **Short**.

Standard deviation (E): A measure of how much the values of something fluctuate around its mean value. Defined as the square root of the **Variance**.

Stock lending: See **Securities lending**.

Stock index future: Future on a stock index, allowing a hedge against, or bet on, a broad equity market movement.

Stock index option: Option on a stock index future.

Stock option: Option on an individual stock.

Street: The "street" is a term for the market, originating as "Wall Street". A US term for market convention, so in the US market is the convention for quoting the price or yield for a particular instrument.

Strike: The strike price or strike rate of an option is the price or rate at which the holder can insist on the underlying transaction being fulfilled.

Strip: A zero-coupon bond which is produced by separating a standard coupon-bearing bond into its constituent principal and interest components. To strip a bond is to separate its principal amount and its coupons and trade each individual cash flow as a separate instrument ("separately traded and registered for interest and principal"). Also, a strip of **Futures** is a series of short-term futures contracts with consecutive delivery dates, which together create the effect of a longer-term instrument (for example, four consecutive three-month futures contracts as a **Hedge** against a one-year swap). A strip of **FRAs** is similar.

Swap: A foreign exchange swap is the purchase of one currency against another for delivery on one date, with a simultaneous sale to reverse the transaction on another value date. See also **Interest rate swap**, **currency swap**.

Swaption: An **Option** on an **Interest rate swap**, **Currency swap**.

Switch: Exchanges of one gilt holding for another, sometimes entered into between the DMO and a GEMM as part of the DMO's secondary market operations.

Synthetic: A package of transactions which is economically equivalent to a different transaction (for example, the purchase of a **Call option** and simultaneous sale of a **Put** option at the same **Strike** is a synthetic **Forward** purchase.)

T

T/N: See **Tom/next**.

Tail: The exposure to interest rates over a forward–forward period arising from a mismatched position (such as a two-month borrowing against a three-month loan). A forward foreign exchange dealer's exposure to **Spot** movements.

Tap: The issue of a gilt for exceptional market management reasons and not on a pre-announced schedule.

Term: The time between the beginning and end of a deal or investment.

Tick: The minimum change allowed in a futures price.

Time deposit: A non-**Negotiable** deposit for a specific term.

Time option: A forward currency deal in which the value date is set to be within a period rather than on a particular day. The customer sets the exact date two working days before settlement.

Time value of money: The concept that a future cash flow can be valued as the amount of money which it is necessary to invest now in order to achieve that cash flow in the future. See **Present value, Future value.**

Today/tomorrow: See **Overnight**.

Tom/next: A transaction from the next working day ("tomorrow") until the day after ("next day" – i.e. **Spot** in the foreign exchange market).

Total return swap: Swap agreement in which the total return of bank loans or credit-sensitive securities is exchanged for some other cash flow usually tied to **LIBOR**, or other loans, or credit-sensitive securities. It allows participants to effectively go **Long** or **Short** the credit risk of the **Underlying** asset.

Traded option: Option that is listed on and cleared by an exchange, with standard terms and delivery months.

Tranche: One of a series of two or more issues with the same coupon rate and maturity date. The tranches become fungible at a future date, usually just after the first coupon date.

Transaction risk: Extent to which the value of transactions that have already been agreed is affected by market risk.

Transparent: A term used to refer to how clear asset prices are in a market. A transparent market is one in which a majority of market participants are aware of what level a particular bond or instrument is trading.

Treasury bill: A short-term security issued by a government, generally with a zero **Coupon**.

U

Uncovered option: When the writer of the option does not own the underlying security. Also known as a **Naked** option.

Undated gilts: Gilts for which there is no final date by which the gilt must be redeemed.

Underlying: The underlying of a futures or option contract is the commodity of financial instrument on which the contract depends. Thus the underlying for a bond option is the bond; the underlying for a short-term interest rate futures contract is typically a three-month deposit.

Underwriting: An arrangement by which a company is guaranteed that an issue of debt (bonds) will raise a given amount of cash. Underwriting is carried out by investment banks, who undertake to purchase any part of the debt issue not taken up by the public. A commission is charged for this service.

V

Value-at-risk (VAR):   Formally, the probabilistic bound of market losses over a given period of time (known as the holding period) expressed in terms of a specified degree of certainty (known as the confidence interval). Put more simply, the VAR is the worst-case loss that would be expected over the holding period within the probability set out by the confidence interval. Larger losses are possible but with a low probability. For instance, a portfolio whose VAR is $20 million over a one-day holding period, with a 95% confidence interval, would have only a 5% chance of suffering an overnight loss greater than $20 million.

Value date: The date on which a deal is to be consummated. In some bond markets, the value date for coupon accruals can sometimes differ from the settlement date.

Vanilla: A vanilla transaction is a straightforward one.

VAR: See **Value-at-risk**.

Variable currency: Exchange rates are quoted in terms of the number of units of one currency (the variable or counter currency) which corresponds to one unit of the other currency (the **Base currency**).

Variance ($E2$):   A measure of how much the values of something fluctuate around its mean value. Defined as the average of (value − mean)2. See **Standard deviation**.

Variance-covariance methodology: Methodology for calculating the **Value-at-risk** of a portfolio as a function of the **Volatility** of each asset or liability position in the portfolio and the correlation between the positions.

Variation margin: The band agreed between the parties to a repo transaction at the outset within which the value of the collateral may fluctuate before triggering a right to call for cash or securities to reinstate the initial margin on the repo transaction.

Vega: The change in an option's value relative to a change in the **Underlying's** volatility.

Volatility: The **Standard deviation** of the continuously compounded return on the **Underlying**. Volatility is generally annualised.

W

Warrant: A security giving the holder a right to subscribe to a share or bond at a given price and from a certain date. If this right is not exercised before the maturity date, the warrant will expire worthless.

Warrant-driven swap: Swap with a warrant attached allowing the issuer of the fixed-rate bond to go on paying a floating rate in the event that they exercise another warrant allowing them to prolong the life of the bond.

When-issued trading: Trading a bond before the issue date; no interest is accrued during this period. Also known as the "grey market".

Write: To sell an option is to write it. The person selling an option is known as the **Writer**.

Writer: The same as "seller" of an **Option**.

X

X: Used to denote the strike price of an option; sometimes this is denoted using the term K.

Y

Yield: The interest rate which can be earned on an investment, currently quoted by the market or implied by the current market price for the investment – as opposed to the **Coupon** paid by an issuer on a security, which is based on the coupon rate and the face value. For a bond, generally the same as yield to maturity unless otherwise specified.

Yield curve: Graphical representation of the maturity structure of interest rates, plotting yields of bonds that are all of the same class or credit quality against the maturity of the bonds.

Yield-curve option: Option that allows purchasers to take a view on a yield curve without having to take a view about a market's direction.

Yield-curve swap: Swap in which the index rates of the two interest streams are at different points on the yield curve. Both payments are refixed with the same frequency whatever the index rate.

Yield to equivalent life: The same as **Yield to maturity** for a bond with partial redemptions.

Yield to maturity: The **Internal rate of return** of a bond – the yield necessary to discount all the bond's cash flows to an **NPV** equal to its current price. See **Simple yield to maturity, Current yield**.

YTM: See **Yield to maturity**.

Z

Zero-coupon: A zero-coupon security is one that does not pay a **Coupon**. Its price is correspondingly less to compensate for this. A zero-coupon **Yield** is the yield which a zero-coupon investment for that term would have if it were consistent with the **Par yield curve**.

Zero-coupon bond: Bond on which no coupon is paid. It is either issued at a discount or redeemed at a premium to face value.

Zero-coupon swap: Swap converting the payment pattern of a zero-coupon bond, either to that of a normal, coupon-paying fixed-rate bond or to a **Floating rate**.